# REVISE BTEC NATIONAL
# Health and Social Care
## UNIT 2

GW00871459

# PRACTICE ASSESSMENTS Plus⁺

Series Consultant: Harry Smith
Author: Elizabeth Haworth

## A note from the publisher

These practice assessments are designed to complement your revision and to help prepare you for the external assessment. They do not include all the content and skills needed for the complete course and have been written to help you practise what you have learned. They may not be representative of a real assessment.

While the publishers have made every attempt to ensure that advice on the qualification and its assessment is accurate, the official specification and associated assessment guidance materials are the only authoritative source of information and should always be referred to for definitive guidance.

This qualification is reviewed on a regular basis and may be updated in the future. Any such updates that affect the content of this book will be outlined at www.pearsonfe.co.uk/BTECchanges

For the full range of Pearson revision titles across KS2, KS3, GCSE, Functional Skills, AS/A Level and BTEC visit:
www.pearsonschools.co.uk/revise

Published by Pearson Education Limited, 80 Strand, London, WC2R ORL.

www.pearsonschoolsandfecolleges.co.uk

Copies of official specifications for all Pearson qualifications may be found on the website: qualifications.pearson.com

Text and illustrations © Pearson Education Ltd 2018

Typeset and illustrated by QBS Learning

Produced by QBS Learning

Cover illustration by Miriam Sturdee

The right of Elizabeth Haworth to be identified as author of this work has been asserted by her in accordance with the Copyright, Designs and Patents Act 1988.

First published 2018

21 20 19 18

10 9 8 7 6 5 4 3 2 1

**British Library Cataloguing in Publication Data**

A catalogue record for this book is available from the British Library

ISBN 978 1 292 25669 6

Printed in Slovakia by Neografia

**Acknowledgements**

The author and publisher would like to thank the following organisation for permission to reproduce text:

Page 5 © Mencap 2018 www.mencap.org.uk/learning-disability-explained/what-learning-disability

**Note from the publisher**

Pearson has robust editorial processes, including answer and fact checks, to ensure the accuracy of the content in this publication, and every effort is made to ensure this publication is free of errors. We are, however, only human, and occasionally errors do occur. Pearson is not liable for any misunderstandings that arise as a result of errors in this publication, but it is our priority to ensure that the content is accurate. If you spot an error, please do contact us at resourcescorrections@pearson.com so we can make sure it is corrected.

**Websites**

Pearson Education Limited is not responsible for the content of any external internet sites. It is essential for tutors to preview each website before using it in class so as to ensure that the URL is still accurate, relevant and appropriate. We suggest that tutors bookmark useful websites and consider enabling learners to access them through the school/college intranet.

# Introduction

This book has been designed to help you to practise the skills you may need for the external assessment of BTEC National Health and Social Care – Unit 2: Working in Health and Social Care. You may be studying this unit as part of the BTEC National Certificate, Extended Certificate, Foundation Diploma, Diploma or Extended Diploma in Health and Social Care.

## About the practice assessments

The book contains four practice assessments for the unit, but, unlike your actual assessment, each question has targeted hints, guidance and support in the margin to help you understand how to tackle it.

 gives you relevant pages in the Pearson Revise BTEC National Health and Social Care Revision Guide so you can revise the essential content. This will also help you to understand how the essential content is applied to different contexts when assessed.

 gets you started and reminds you of the skills or knowledge you need to apply.

 helps you think about how to approach a question, such as making a brief plan.

 provides content that you need to learn such as a definition, rule or formula.

 reminds you of content related to the question to aid your revision on that topic.

 helps you avoid common pitfalls.

 appears in the final practice assessment and helps you become familiar with answering in a given time, and thinking about allocating appropriate time for different kinds of questions.

There is space within the book for you to write your answers to the questions. However, if you are planning or writing notes, or simply require more space to complete your answers, you may want to use separate paper.

There is also an answer section at the back of the book, so you can check your answers for each practice assessment.

## Check the Pearson website

For overarching guidance on the official assessment outcomes and key terms used in your assessment, please refer to the specification on the Pearson website.

The practice questions, support and answers in this book are provided to help you to revise the essential content in the specification, and to help you review ways of applying your skills. The details of your actual assessment may change, so always make sure you are up to date on its format and requirements by asking your tutor, or checking the Pearson website, for the most up-to-date Sample Assessment Material, mark schemes and any past papers.

# Contents

### A small bit of small print

Pearson publishes Sample Assessment Material and the Specification on its website. This is the official content and this book should be used in conjunction with it. The questions have been written to help you test your knowledge and skills. Remember: the real assessment may not look like this.

# Practice assessment 1

## SECTION A

**Revision Guide**
pages 58, 59,
61, 62 and 98

> **Answer ALL questions.**
> **Write your answers in the spaces provided.**

**1**

### Scenario 1: Ill health

Nigel is 45 years old. A brain injury has left him partially paralysed down his right-hand side, after a year in hospital, initially on a medical ward and then in a rehabilitation centre. He will be on medication for his brain injury for the rest of his life.

He now walks with the aid of a stick, swinging his right leg to walk and cannot move his right arm at all. He lives on his own in a new home and has been allocated a support worker, Tama, to help him adjust to his condition. He has family and friends living close by.

Nigel is depressed. He suffers from mood swings and is often angry with his situation, although he pretends to be cheerful and makes fun of himself and his condition when he is with family and friends.

(a) Identify **two** ways in which a support worker might help Nigel adapt to his changed circumstances.

1 ...................................................................................................................

...................................................................................................................

2 ...................................................................................................................

...................................................................................................................

**2 marks**

**Hint**

For this **identify** question, you simply need to provide the facts asked for, with no added details.

**Hint**

Imagine what you would need help with if you were partially paralysed down one side and lived on your own.

**Hint**

Remember that not only will Nigel need help doing day-to-day tasks, but he will also need help to come to terms with his changed life. His family and friends will need support with this too.

**Revision Guide**
pages 65, 66, 67, 68 and 70

**Hint**

To answer this **describe** question, you need to give two care values, such as 'empower him', or 'keep him safe', and add some detail for each about how the support worker can do this.

**Hint**

Although there are many ways in which a support worker can empower an individual, this question asks you to consider **two** of the care values, so only give one answer about empowering Nigel. Your second answer should be about a different care value such as ensuring safety.

**LEARN IT!**

**Empower** means giving an individual information and support so they can make informed decisions and choices about their life in order to live as independently as possible.

(b) Describe how his support worker might apply **two** of the care values when helping Nigel.

1 ................................................................................................................

................................................................................................................

................................................................................................................

................................................................................................................

2 ................................................................................................................

................................................................................................................

................................................................................................................

................................................................................................................

**4 marks**

(c) Explain how healthcare service providers can help Nigel now he has left hospital.

..............................................................................................................

..............................................................................................................

..............................................................................................................

..............................................................................................................

..............................................................................................................

..............................................................................................................

..............................................................................................................

..............................................................................................................

..............................................................................................................

..............................................................................................................

..............................................................................................................

**6 marks**

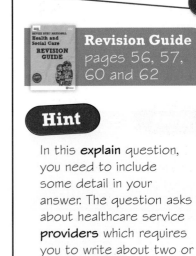

**Revision Guide**
pages 56, 57, 60 and 62

**Hint**

In this **explain** question, you need to include some detail in your answer. The question asks about healthcare service **providers** which requires you to write about two or more services.

**Hint**

The number of marks available should guide you on the amount of detail to include in your answer. For 6 marks, you could identify two healthcare service providers and give at least two examples of how each can help Nigel. Alternatively, you could identify three healthcare service providers and include one way in which each can help him.

**Watch out!**

The question asks about healthcare service providers, so you won't gain any marks if you write about any social care services.

**Revision Guide**
pages 75, 92, 93 and 94

### Hint

This is a **discuss** question, so make sure you add some detail about each of the concerns you write about.

### Watch out!

Make sure you include a range of ways the employer will ensure Tama meets professional standards while staying safe.

It is easy to focus solely on one way, such as providing policies and codes of practice, and then writing lots of different examples, but this will limit the mark you are awarded.

### Hint

Try to include at least four different ways with some added detail about each one.

### Hint

You don't need to name any organisations or regulatory bodies but you should think about the responsibilities the organisation has towards both Nigel and the support worker.

(d) Discuss how the organisation which employs Tama, Nigel's support worker, will ensure she meets professional standards while staying safe herself.

.......................................................................................................................

.......................................................................................................................

.......................................................................................................................

.......................................................................................................................

.......................................................................................................................

.......................................................................................................................

.......................................................................................................................

.......................................................................................................................

.......................................................................................................................

.......................................................................................................................

.......................................................................................................................

.......................................................................................................................

.......................................................................................................................

.......................................................................................................................

.......................................................................................................................

.......................................................................................................................

8 marks

Total for Question 1 = 20 marks

# SECTION B

Revision Guide
page 97

**2**

**Scenario 2: Learning disability**

Owen is 22 years old, is strong and physically fit, and has a learning disability. He still lives with his parents and during the week attends a day centre for people with learning disabilities.

Owen's parents hope that one day he will be able to live independently as they are in their late 50s: they worry about how he will cope when they are no longer able to care for him. He has two brothers and two sisters but they all live in different parts of the country and have busy lives.

(a) Identify **two** skills the day centre could teach Owen to help prepare him for living independently.

1  .............................................................................................................

.............................................................................................................

2  .............................................................................................................

.............................................................................................................

**2 marks**

**Hint**

For this **identify** question, you simply need to state two different skills that will help Owen to live independently.

**Hint**

Imagine you are going to live in your own flat away from your parents for the first time. What will you need to be able to do to look after yourself?

**LEARN IT!**

Mencap defines a **learning difficulty** as 'a reduced intellectual ability and difficulty with everyday activities [...] which affects someone for their whole life.' (Source: MENCAP)

**Revision Guide**
page 97

**Hint**

This is a **describe** question, so make sure you add some detail about each of the concerns you write about.

**Prepare**

Before you begin your answer, you can plan your writing by imagining you are looking after a 22-year-old man with learning difficulties – write a bullet list of concerns you may have. For example, how might he behave if he doesn't understand something and gets frustrated?

**Hint**

Think about what you know about care values, especially the one about empowerment, as the day centre is trying to help Owen live independently in the community.

(b) Describe **two** concerns the day centre may have when providing care for Owen.

1 ................................................................................

................................................................................

................................................................................

................................................................................

2 ................................................................................

................................................................................

................................................................................

................................................................................

4 marks

(c) Explain how an advocate may be of use to Owen when he moves into his own accommodation in the community.

.........................................................................................................

.........................................................................................................

.........................................................................................................

.........................................................................................................

.........................................................................................................

.........................................................................................................

.........................................................................................................

.........................................................................................................

.........................................................................................................

.........................................................................................................

.........................................................................................................

6 marks

**Revision Guide**
pages 86 and 97

**Hint**

For this **explain** question, you need to say how an advocate can support Owen and add some detail to each example. Be guided by the number of marks available, e.g. you could give three different examples and add some detail for each.

**Hint**

Think about how your parents or guardians supported you when you were young. Did they speak up for you? Why? In what circumstances?

**LEARN IT!**

An **advocate** speaks on behalf of someone else who has communication difficulties, to represent their interests.

**Revision Guide**
pages 67, 72
and 97

### Hint

For this **discuss** question, you need to consider the different ways in which organisations keep service users safe and include some detail for each.

### Prepare

Before you start to write, make some notes of what you want to include in your answer. You could draw a mind map or note down a list of bullet points – whatever works best for you.

### Hint

You are only required to write about ensuring safety. Discussing other care values will not gain you any extra marks, unless you make it clear how they are related to ensuring safety. For example, protecting Owen from discrimination is keeping him safe if that discrimination means that Owen is being abused or is at risk of physical harm.

(d) Discuss how managers and carers at the day centre can keep Owen safe.

..............................................................................................................................

..............................................................................................................................

..............................................................................................................................

..............................................................................................................................

..............................................................................................................................

..............................................................................................................................

..............................................................................................................................

..............................................................................................................................

..............................................................................................................................

..............................................................................................................................

..............................................................................................................................

..............................................................................................................................

..............................................................................................................................

..............................................................................................................................

**8 marks**

**Total for Question 2 = 20 marks**

# SECTION C

Revision Guide
pages 58, 62,
64 and 98

**3**

**Scenario 3: Physical/sensory disability**

Angie is 55 years old, lives in London and has a visual impairment. Her parents and one of her brothers lost their sight due to an inherited condition and she has now started to lose hers. Although she knew this could happen, she is struggling to come to terms with the fact that she is going blind.

Angie is learning to read Braille but, because she is doing this in middle adulthood, she is finding it difficult and keeps saying she is going to give up. Her husband, Steve, is very supportive and is encouraging her to continue to learn Braille.

She will be allocated a social worker to help her and hopes to have a guide dog one day, like her parents and brother do.

(a) Identify **two** ways in which the social worker can support Angie as she loses her sight.

1 ...............................................................................................................

...............................................................................................................

2 ...............................................................................................................

...............................................................................................................

2 marks

**Hint**

For this **identify** question, you only need to state the two facts asked for, without adding any detail.

**Hint**

Think about your day-to-day life. What might you find it hard to do if you could no longer see?

**Hint**

Show that you understand what support Angie will need from the social worker by thinking of two ideas of your own. Do not include learning to read Braille (her husband is supporting her with that) and do not include putting her in contact with the Guide Dogs for the Blind (because her family will give her that information).

**Watch out!**

Make sure you do not confuse the role of a social worker with that of a support worker. A support worker is more 'hands on', supporting people with their day-to-day living by helping them put into practice the solutions to problems suggested by a social worker. This question is about a social worker.

**Revision Guide**
pages 69 and 70

**Hint**

For this **describe** question, you need to add more detail than you would when answering an 'identify' question.

**Hint**

Try to include four relevant points to gain a good mark.

**Hint**

Think about the precautions you take to keep your mobile phone and other devices such as iPads secure.

**Explore**

The Data Protection Act 2018, which supplements the EU General Data Protection Regulation (GDPR), came into force on 25 May 2018. This superseded the Data Protection Act 1998. It is the biggest change to data protection legislation since 1998, introducing new requirements for how all organisations process personal data. It is important to know about the change.

(b) Describe how the social worker will keep personal information about Angie secure.

...............................................................................................................................

...............................................................................................................................

...............................................................................................................................

...............................................................................................................................

...............................................................................................................................

...............................................................................................................................

...............................................................................................................................

...............................................................................................................................

**4 marks**

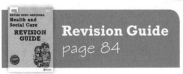
(c) Explain **three** barriers that Angie may face when accessing services, such as when visiting her GP, dentist or optician.

..............................................................................................

..............................................................................................

..............................................................................................

..............................................................................................

..............................................................................................

..............................................................................................

..............................................................................................

..............................................................................................

..............................................................................................

..............................................................................................

..............................................................................................

6 marks

**Revision Guide**
*page 84*

**Hint**

For this **explain** question, you need to identify three barriers and add some detail about each one.

**Hint**

Think about how you would try to access your GP if you were blind. How would you make and record the appointment? How would you get there and back? How would you cope when you got there?

**Watch out!**

This question does not ask you to suggest ways to overcome any barriers you identify. If you do you will not gain any extra marks.

**Revision Guide**
pages 88 and 91

**Revision Guide**
pages 88 and 91

**Hint**

For this **discuss** question, you need to identify two organisations that regulate and inspect social care services. You also need to include some detail about how they do this.

**Hint**

The organisations that you have learned about regulate and inspect all health and social care services, not only social care, so you can just refer to services in your answer.

**LEARN IT!**

**Regulate** means to lay down guidelines and codes of practice that must be followed by service providers.

**Inspect** means to examine the performance of organisations against a set of standards and report the results to the public.

**Watch out!**

The scenario tells you that Angie lives in London. This means you need to know and write about the organisations that regulate and inspect care providers in England.

(d) Discuss the roles of **two** organisations which regulate and inspect social care services in England.

....................................................................................................................

....................................................................................................................

....................................................................................................................

....................................................................................................................

....................................................................................................................

....................................................................................................................

....................................................................................................................

....................................................................................................................

....................................................................................................................

....................................................................................................................

....................................................................................................................

....................................................................................................................

....................................................................................................................

....................................................................................................................

8 marks

Total for Question 3 = 20 marks

# SECTION D

**Revision Guide**
page 100

**Scenario 4: Age-related needs (later adulthood)**

Shama is 87 years old. She lives at home with her family and is fit and healthy, having stayed active all her life.

She had a fall and fractured her pelvis, so was admitted to hospital, where she had an operation. She was then cared for in hospital, before being moved to a nursing home to continue her recuperation.

You are a trainee healthcare assistant in the nursing home and Shama is one of the patients you help care for.

(a) Identify **two** rights relating to Shama that you need to be aware of when caring for her.

1 ................................................................................................................

................................................................................................................

2 ................................................................................................................

................................................................................................................

2 marks

**Hint**

For this **identify** question, you don't need to include any detail beyond stating two of Shama's rights.

**Hint**

If you can't think of any rights relating to Shama, think about how you would expect to be treated if you were in hospital.

**Revision Guide**
pages 75, 81
and 93

### Hint

For this **describe** question, you need to include some detail about each point you make.

### Hint

The question asks you to describe how your skills will be both monitored and improved, so make sure you write about both in your answer.

### Hint

Answer the question as though you are describing how this happens to **you**, not as though you are talking about **any** trainee healthcare assistant.

### Watch out!

This question is about skills, which are abilities to do certain things, rather than qualities, which are attributes possessed by a person, such as being kind or polite. One skill you might use as a healthcare assistant looking after Shama is to help her move from her bed to a chair; another is to help her wash and dress.

(b) Describe how your professional skills will be monitored and improved by your line manager.

.............................................................................................

.............................................................................................

.............................................................................................

.............................................................................................

.............................................................................................

.............................................................................................

.............................................................................................

**4 marks**

(c) Explain what your role as a healthcare assistant involves.

.............................................................................................................................

.............................................................................................................................

.............................................................................................................................

.............................................................................................................................

.............................................................................................................................

.............................................................................................................................

.............................................................................................................................

.............................................................................................................................

.............................................................................................................................

.............................................................................................................................

.............................................................................................................................

**6 marks**

**Revision Guide**
pages 56, 60, 75, 93, 95 and 100

**Hint**

For this **explain** question, you need to give examples of what a healthcare assistant does, and include some detail with each example. If you are finding it hard to think of examples, you could imagine what you would need help with if you had limited mobility after a fall and were in hospital. (A hospital is another place where healthcare assistants work.)

**Hint**

Use the number of marks available as a guide to how many healthcare assistant's duties you should write about.

**Revision Guide**
pages 73, 74
and 77

### Hint

For this **discuss** question, you need to consider different aspects of partnership working, and include some detail with each example. Try to justify why each aspect of partnership working will be good for Shama and her family.

### Hint

Use the number of marks available to guide your answer. You could write about at least four different aspects of partnership working and explain how each is beneficial to Shama and her family.

### Watch out!

This question asks you to discuss **benefits** of partnership working so, even if you know some disadvantages of partnership working, do not include them as they will not gain you any marks.

### Watch out!

Don't forget to link the different aspects of multidisciplinary working to Shama and her family, rather than talking about the general benefits of multidisciplinary working.

### Hint

If you have time, remember to check your writing and spelling. Poor spelling and grammar can make it hard to understand what you're trying to say.

(d) Discuss how multidisciplinary working can benefit Shama and her family.

..................................................................................................

..................................................................................................

..................................................................................................

..................................................................................................

..................................................................................................

..................................................................................................

..................................................................................................

..................................................................................................

..................................................................................................

..................................................................................................

..................................................................................................

..................................................................................................

..................................................................................................

..................................................................................................

..................................................................................................

8 marks

Total for Question 4 = 20 marks

**TOTAL FOR PAPER = 80 MARKS**

# Practice assessment 2

## SECTION A

Answer ALL questions.
Write your answers in the spaces provided.

 Revision Guide
pages 95
and 99

### Scenario 1: Ill health

Ava is 8 years old and has leukaemia, a cancer of the blood. She is currently in a children's hospital and is being cared for by a team of staff made up of people with different roles. They are confident that Ava will make a full recovery as her condition has been diagnosed early. However, the treatment will last for months or even years, so she will be away from her family, friends, home and school for a long time. Although her family visit every day and make sure friends keep in touch, she is aware that home and school life is continuing without her, so is often sad.

Although her ward has a teacher, Ava is often very tired (a side effect of the treatment) so she doesn't always feel like doing school work. Like other children in her position she is falling behind her classmates. She has a paediatric nurse, Sally, who works closely with both her and her family.

**Hint**

For this **identify** question, you only need to provide the facts asked for, with no added details.

**Hint**

Imagine someone you are close to is ill in hospital. What support would you like a nurse to offer you? Would you like to be clear about exactly what was happening to your relative or friend?

**LEARN IT!**

The word **paediatric** means of, or relating to, the medical care of children.

(a) Identify **two** ways in which Sally can support Ava's family.

1 Sally should make sure to keep the family informed and updated about her condition ✗

2 Sally should talk to the family about a plan and a support system for the family ✓    **2 marks**    ①

① reassure and comfort them

**Watch out!**

This question is about Ava's family, so you won't get any marks if you write about ways Sally can support Ava herself.

**Revision Guide** pages 56, 60, 67, 70, 72 and 95

**Hint**

To answer this question you need to think about how Sally can protect Ava from any risk of harm, for example, by making sure all visitors use the hand gel provided on the ward to prevent infection.

**Hint**

For this **describe** question, you need to identify two ways in which Sally can safeguard Ava and to add some detail about each of these ways. For example, if you write about making sure all equipment is sterile, explain that this is to reduce the risk of infection.

**LEARN IT!**

To **safeguard** a child means to promote their wellbeing and protect them from harm, to both their health and development, so providing safe and effective care.

(b) Describe **two** ways that Sally can safeguard Ava in the hospital ward.

1 By monitoring and checking up on her, by talking and asking her questions X keep avas records secure so no one can access them if they aren't meant to.

2 asking her what she wants, if she feels safe, what she can do to make her bed more comfortable X making sure all equipment is sterile and bedding is clean due to risk of infection.

**4 marks**

18

**Revision Guide**
pages 56, 60
and 79

(c) Explain the roles of **three** other professionals who will help Ava while she is in hospital.

1 Support worker, to offer support or therapy, advice and checking up to see what (can) he (become)

2 teacher, she will help with Avas education as she wont be attending school ✗

3 doctor, to monitor treatment, make sure all is going as planned. ✓

6 marks

④

**Hint**

For this **explain** question, you should include some detail in your answers. You will have learned about the roles of some professionals in your lessons. If you can't remember three, but you know of others through personal experience, or from watching television programmes, it is fine to include them.

**Hint**

As this question is worth 6 marks you should identify three professionals and write at least one example of what each of their roles involves.

**Watch out!**

The word 'other' in the question tells you that you should not describe the role of the paediatric nurse or the ward teacher mentioned in the scenario. The word 'professionals' means that you should write about people who are trained and paid to work at the hospital, rather than volunteers such as hospital visitors.

**Watch out!**

Remember that this question is about roles, **not** responsibilities. A role is a description of what a person does within their job, whereas a responsibility is a duty to make sure a particular task is done to the required standard, for example, by following policies and procedures in the workplace.

**Revision Guide**
page 75

**Hint**

In this **describe** question, you need to state two of the line manager's responsibilities and add some detail to show that you understand what a line manager does.

**Watch out!**

This question is not asking you about the support worker allegedly slapping Janny. It is asking how a line manager who has responsibility for other workers ensures that those workers are delivering quality care.

**LEARN IT!**

A **line manager** not only oversees someone else's work but also takes action, depending on the standard of this work.

---

Janny tells his social worker, Linwood, that his support worker isn't very nice to him, disclosing that she sometimes loses her temper with him and slaps him. The social worker monitors the situation and overhears the support worker telling Janny that she doesn't like him because he is Polish.

(b) Describe **two** day-to-day responsibilities of the support worker's line manager to ensure that workers are delivering care to the required standards.

1  to moniter these support workers and to ask people like Jane if they are comfortable with there support worker ✗

2  line manager should make sure addaqate care and standards are met ✓✓

4 marks

(c) Explain the roles of **three** other professionals who will help Ava while she is in hospital.

1 Support worker, to offer support or therapy, advice and checking up to see what (care) he income

2 Teacher, she will help with Ava's education as she won't be attending school ✗

3 doctor, to monitor treatments make sure all is going as planned. ✓

6 marks

④

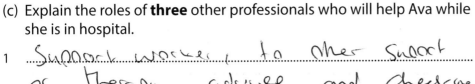 
**Revision Guide**
pages 56, 60 and 79

**Hint**

For this **explain** question, you should include some detail in your answers. You will have learned about the roles of some professionals in your lessons. If you can't remember three, but you know of others through personal experience, or from watching television programmes, it is fine to include them.

**Hint**

As this question is worth 6 marks you should identify three professionals and write at least one example of what each of their roles involves.

**Watch out!**

The word 'other' in the question tells you that you should not describe the role of the paediatric nurse or the ward teacher mentioned in the scenario. The word 'professionals' means that you should write about people who are trained and paid to work at the hospital, rather than volunteers such as hospital visitors.

**Watch out!**

Remember that this question is about roles, **not** responsibilities. A role is a description of what a person does within their job, whereas a responsibility is a duty to make sure a particular task is done to the required standard, for example, by following policies and procedures in the workplace.

**Revision Guide**
pages 92, 93,
101 and 102

**Hint**

For this **discuss** question,
you need to write about
different ways in which
healthcare professionals
gain and maintain their
skills, knowledge and
understanding.

**Hint**

You also need to think
about how healthcare
professionals can make
sure their working
practices are of a high
standard, so they do
not adversely affect
the people who use the
hospital services.

**Hint**

You could structure your
answer in four parts:

1. How healthcare
   professionals train
   before they get the job.

2. What they do when
   they start the job.

3. How they train on
   the job.

4. How they make sure
   their working practices
   stay at a high standard.

(d) Discuss how the healthcare professionals who work in an NHS
hospital train for their roles and maintain their own good working
practices.

> health care proffesionals can be
> start training from going college
> doing a health and soccal cant
> course, many on to uni or
> apprenticship. doing social work such
> as teaching or going into nursing
> care or care work
>
> they will most likey shaddow
> someone then be shadowed so they
> know and learn what they are doing
> and how to do certain things then
> be shadowed to show their work
> today and to keep there standard up
> they should be checked in on
> others now and then to make sure
> standard is kept
>
> read articles
> keep up to date with
> changes and policies.    ③    8 marks

**Total for Question 1 = 20 marks**

# SECTION B

**Revision Guide**
pages 58, 59, 61 and 63

**Scenario 2: Learning disability**

Janny is 19 years old and has Down's syndrome. He lives in a residential unit for people with learning disabilities where he can learn life skills to help him get a job. At the unit he has a support worker. He also has a social worker, Linwood, who calls in regularly to see him and his parents.

Janny is very affectionate, helpful and keen to please everyone. He has recently met Rosie at the unit, who is his age. She also has learning difficulties and is now his girlfriend. Janny's parents like Rosie but are concerned about their relationship.

(a) Identify **two** ways in which Janny's social worker can address his parents' concerns.

1 .....They should tell the parents about the rules and protection in place for relationship...

2 .....by talking to Rosie and Janny making sure they understand certain things....

②   2 marks

**Hint**

For this **identify** question, you simply need to state two ways in which the social worker can help with this situation, without adding any detail.

**Hint**

Think about who the social worker should speak to. Janny? Rosie? Together? Apart? The other staff? What should the social worker say?

21

**Revision Guide**
page 75

**Hint**

In this **describe** question, you need to state two of the line manager's responsibilities and add some detail to show that you understand what a line manager does.

**Watch out!**

This question is not asking you about the support worker allegedly slapping Janny. It is asking how a line manager who has responsibility for other workers ensures that those workers are delivering quality care.

**LEARN IT!**

A **line manager** not only oversees someone else's work but also takes action, depending on the standard of this work.

---

Janny tells his social worker, Linwood, that his support worker isn't very nice to him, disclosing that she sometimes loses her temper with him and slaps him. The social worker monitors the situation and overhears the support worker telling Janny that she doesn't like him because he is Polish.

(b) Describe **two** day-to-day responsibilities of the support worker's line manager to ensure that workers are delivering care to the required standards.

1 to monitor these support workers and to ask people like Jang if they are comfortable with these support worker ✗

2 line manager should make sure addquate care and standards are met ✓✓

③

**4 marks**

(c) Explain how the social worker should tackle Janny's claims that his support worker isn't very nice to him and sometimes slaps him.

By asking other people what, that, Support worker has if she is meeting being professional and if they are happy and get along with her. to g to do men Social worker (have) talk to Danys Parents, and the residentil units and Jannys friends to see if Janny has told anyone else, monitor Janny for any brusing or marks.  ①

① speak to Janny with parents present

② suspend support worker while the investigation goes on

③ interview the social worker and ask for their account, start from beginning.

6 marks

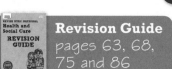
**Revision Guide**
pages 63, 68, 75 and 86

**Hint**

For this **explain** question, you are required to mention each of the various stages of pursuing Janny's claim of being abused.

**Hint**

To gain a good mark you need to mention the different people the social worker should speak to in order to investigate this allegation. You also need to write about what happens following on from the investigation.

**Hint**

Use the number of marks available to guide your answer and how much information you should provide.

**Explore**

Supporters of complaints and whistleblowing policies say they help maintain best practice. Do you think they represent the interests of both service users and service providers?

**Revision Guide**
pages 87, 88,
89 and 90

### Hint

For this **discuss** question, you need to mention which body would carry out the inspection (in the area where you live), and then write about the stages of the inspection.

### Prepare

Before you start your answer, you could write a broad plan in the form of a few bullets listing what happens when a residential unit is inspected. In this way, you're likely to cover everything you want to say.

### Hint

Your answer should include the name of the professional body as well as the inspection steps.

### Hint

Make sure you include what happens with the outcome of the inspection process.

---

(d) Discuss how a residential unit is externally inspected.

① Identify the scope and purpose of the investigation.

② observes service delivery

③ rates the service and publishes findings.

④ Take action to improve services and protected services users where needed.

8 marks

**Total for Question 2 = 20 marks**

# SECTION C

## Scenario 3: Physical/sensory disability

Taj is 45 years old and married with three children. Last year he was the victim of a serious car crash and, in order to save his life, paramedics had to amputate his arm at the scene of the crash. He also suffered injuries, which left him with a scarred face and a limp.

He lives at home with his family, who are very supportive. He is waiting to be fitted with a prosthetic arm.

Before the accident he was very outgoing and loved playing sports, but now his self-esteem is low and he has become withdrawn, resentful and depressed. When he goes to medical appointments he is aware of people looking at him.

His wife is concerned about his state of mind, so has contacted a charity which supports the victims of road accidents. She has persuaded him to call their telephone helpline.

(a) Identify **two** ways in which Taj could be supported by this type of charity.

1 .................................................................................................................................

.................................................................................................................................

2 .................................................................................................................................

.................................................................................................................................

2 marks

**Revision Guide**
pages 78
and 98

**Hint**

This is an **identify** question, so you only need to state the two ways asked for, without adding any detail.

**Hint**

Think about how you would feel if you suddenly lost an arm and were facially scarred. What support would you need? Why might it not be enough to have your family supporting you?

**Explore**

Helplines are staffed mainly by trained volunteers. Many of them know people who have been affected by the issues which the charity seeks to address. How might this help both the volunteers and those phoning the helpline?

**Revision Guide**
pages 56
and 60

**Hint**

This is a **describe** question, so it requires you to add more detail than an identify question.

**Hint**

To gain high marks, try to include four relevant points.

**Hint**

Think about how you would cope if you only had one arm. What practical help would you need?

**Watch out!**

This question is about practical solutions to physical problems rather than any emotional support.

(b) Describe how an occupational therapist could help Taj be physically able to tackle day-to-day tasks.

......................................................................................................

......................................................................................................

......................................................................................................

......................................................................................................

......................................................................................................

......................................................................................................

......................................................................................................

4 marks

(c) Explain how the occupational therapist can empower Taj.

..................................................................................................................................

..................................................................................................................................

..................................................................................................................................

..................................................................................................................................

..................................................................................................................................

..................................................................................................................................

..................................................................................................................................

..................................................................................................................................

..................................................................................................................................

..................................................................................................................................

..................................................................................................................................

..................................................................................................................................

6 marks

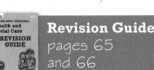

**Revision Guide**
pages 65
and 66

**Hint**

In this **explain** question, you need to identify ways in which Taj will be empowered and add some detail about each one.

**Hint**

As this question is worth 6 marks you should identify three ways Taj can be empowered and add at least one piece of detail to each. If you can only think of two ways you will need to add at least two pieces of detail to each to gain a good mark.

**Hint**

Reflect on how you have felt when you have been unable to do what you want to do (you may have been ill or had a broken limb). How did you feel when you got your independence back?

**LEARN IT!**

**Empowerment** means giving individuals information and support, so they can take informed decisions and make choices about their lives in order to live as independently as possible.

**Revision Guide**
page 74

**Hint**

For this **discuss** question, you need to identify ways in which a holistic approach will help Taj, and also include some detail about how each will benefit him.

**Hint**

To structure your answer, start by saying what a holistic approach is. You then need to show that you understand exactly what this means.

**Hint**

Show your understanding by identifying the additional ways in which Taj will be helped if his care goes beyond his physical injuries, and give some detail as to how each will benefit him. If you do this well, you will only need to include four different aspects and four pieces of added detail, one for each aspect but, to ensure high marks, include more if you have time.

**Hint**

This question refers to all relevant health and social care services, **not** social **or** healthcare services, so you can just refer to services in your answer.

(d) Discuss how services taking a holistic approach to Taj's care will benefit, and so promote, his health and wellbeing.

......................................................................................................................

......................................................................................................................

......................................................................................................................

......................................................................................................................

......................................................................................................................

......................................................................................................................

......................................................................................................................

......................................................................................................................

......................................................................................................................

......................................................................................................................

......................................................................................................................

......................................................................................................................

......................................................................................................................

......................................................................................................................

**8 marks**

**Total for Question 3 = 20 marks**

# SECTION D

**Revision Guide**
pages 82
and 103

**Scenario 4: Age-related needs (later adulthood)**

Charles is 75 years old. He has lived on his own since his wife died four years ago. He recently suffered a fall in which he broke both of his wrists. Although he is otherwise fit and healthy, now he cannot do everyday tasks such as going to the toilet, and washing and feeding himself. Charles books into a retirement home for a week of respite care, where he is rude and abusive towards the staff.

You are a care assistant there and quite like Charles. You suspect his behaviour is due to the embarrassment of having 'women' he doesn't know looking after his personal needs.

Three months later Charles returns, having had another fall and breaking a leg and an arm this time. He has been diagnosed with osteoporosis. You overhear two other care assistants talking about him, and are horrified to hear them planning to get their own back on him by not answering his bell when he rings in the night. One of these care assistants is a good friend of the manager.

(a) Identify **two** ways in which Charles will be vulnerable if his bell is ignored in the night.

1 ...........................................................................................................................

...........................................................................................................................

2 ...........................................................................................................................

...........................................................................................................................

`2 marks`

**Hint**

For this **identify** question, you are not required to include any detail beyond stating the facts asked for.

**Hint**

If you can't think of any ways Charles will be vulnerable, imagine what might happen if he wants to get out of bed to use the toilet in the night.

**LEARN IT!**

**Vulnerable** means Charles is unable to take care of himself and unable to protect himself against significant harm or exploitation.

**Revision Guide**
pages 75
and 94

**Hint**

For this **describe** question, you need to include some detail about each point you make.

**Hint**

The question asks you to describe both how you would implement the policy and how you should expect to be treated, so make sure you include both in your answer.

**Hint**

Answer the question as though you are the care assistant implementing the whistleblowing policy. Start sentences by writing: 'I would report...', 'I would expect...', etc.

(b) Describe how you would implement a whistleblowing policy in this situation and how you should expect to be treated by the manager.

..................................................................................................................................

..................................................................................................................................

..................................................................................................................................

..................................................................................................................................

..................................................................................................................................

..................................................................................................................................

..................................................................................................................................

4 marks

(c) Explain how the care assistants involved could have dealt with the situation better, as they obviously feel that Charles is not treating them with respect.

.......................................................................................................................

.......................................................................................................................

.......................................................................................................................

.......................................................................................................................

.......................................................................................................................

.......................................................................................................................

.......................................................................................................................

.......................................................................................................................

.......................................................................................................................

.......................................................................................................................

.......................................................................................................................

.......................................................................................................................

6 marks

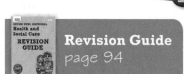

**Revision Guide**
page 94

### Hint

For this **explain** question, you need to think about the possible steps the care assistants could take to complain about Charles's abusive attitude. Add some detail for each step you write about.

### Hint

Make sure you explain at least three steps and include some detail for each in your answer to gain a good mark. If you can't think of much detail, include more steps.

### Hint

If you can't think of how the care assistants should complain, look at a step-by-step complaints procedure for service users, either online or from your own setting. The same procedure applies to service providers.

**Revision Guide**
pages 58, 62,
67 and 70

### Hint

For this **discuss** question,
you need to consider
different aspects of being
a care assistant, and
include some detail for
each responsibility you
identify.

### Prepare

If time allows, make a plan
by noting down bullet
points which outline your
responsibilities. When you
write your answer in full,
you can tick the bullets
off to make sure you have
covered everything you
want to include.

### Watch out!

Remember that this
question is about you
being a care assistant,
so talk about the
responsibilities as though
they are yours.

(d) Discuss your responsibilities as a care assistant looking after the
service users in your care.

.......................................................................................................................

.......................................................................................................................

.......................................................................................................................

.......................................................................................................................

.......................................................................................................................

.......................................................................................................................

.......................................................................................................................

.......................................................................................................................

.......................................................................................................................

.......................................................................................................................

.......................................................................................................................

.......................................................................................................................

.......................................................................................................................

.......................................................................................................................

8 marks

Total for Question 4 = 20 marks

**TOTAL FOR PAPER = 80 MARKS**

# Practice assessment 3

## SECTION A

Answer ALL questions.
Write your answers in the spaces provided.

Revision Guide
page 96

### Scenario 1: Ill health

Beth is 22 years old, a trainee manager in a bank and has mental ill health. She is friendly and bubbly, and everyone comments on what a lovely person she is. However, since she sat her exams at the age of 18, she has struggled with anxiety, finding it hard to sleep for more than a few hours a night, feeling low and becoming easily upset. She has only recently seen a doctor after her parents became concerned and persuaded her to do so.

She has been diagnosed with depression and mild OCD (obsessive compulsive disorder), which in her case takes the form of spending hours worrying about anything that goes wrong, such as relationship breakdowns or her friends letting her down. Although she is intelligent and has a loving and supportive family, she has low self-esteem and feels that nothing goes right for her, expecting things to go wrong before they have even started.

(a) Identify **two** reasons why Beth and her family may not have realised she needed medical help when she was 18.

1 ..........................................................................................................................................

..........................................................................................................................................

2 ..........................................................................................................................................

..........................................................................................................................................

2 marks

**Hint**

For this **identify** question, you only need to provide the facts asked for, without adding any detail.

**Hint**

Think about people you know who have depression or other forms of mental ill health. This could be someone you know personally or someone you have seen on television or on the internet. Is it always easy to see that they have these issues?

**Explore**

Have you, or anyone else you know, had any of the symptoms described? Does this necessarily mean that you or they have mental health issues?

**Revision Guide**
page 96

## Hint

For this **describe** question, you need to identify two strategies Beth's GP can suggest, and also add some detail about how each of those two strategies may help Beth.

## Hint

To answer this question you need to think about how Beth might feel when your strategies are suggested. Telling her to 'pull herself together' or think about others less fortunate than herself won't help, because she won't be able to see beyond her own problems, due to her depression. (It could even make her feel worse.)

## LEARN IT!

People who suffer from **depression** are often unable to cope with day-to-day life, may experience feelings of worthlessness and may have suicidal thoughts. It can be a chronic condition, or it may be short-term due to life circumstances at the time, such as the death of a loved one.

## Watch out!

The question asks for strategies which do **not** involve other health and social care services, so you will not get any marks for suggesting, for example, seeing a counsellor.

(b) Describe two strategies Beth's GP can suggest to help Beth improve her mental health, which do not involve other health and social care services.

1 ...................................................................................................................

...................................................................................................................

...................................................................................................................

...................................................................................................................

2 ...................................................................................................................

...................................................................................................................

...................................................................................................................

...................................................................................................................

4 marks

(c) Explain the roles of at least two service providers who could help
Beth with her depression and OCD.

..................................................................................................................

..................................................................................................................

..................................................................................................................

..................................................................................................................

..................................................................................................................

..................................................................................................................

..................................................................................................................

..................................................................................................................

..................................................................................................................

..................................................................................................................

..................................................................................................................

6 marks

**Revision Guide**
pages 56, 60,
77, 78, 85
and 96

**Hint**

For this **explain** question,
you need to include some
detail in your answers.

**Hint**

As this question is worth
6 marks, you could either
identify two service
providers and write at
least two examples of
how each could help Beth,
or identify three service
providers and write at
least one example for each.

**Hint**

The question asks about
service providers. This
means that you could
write about public-sector
services and/or private and
voluntary services.

**Revision Guide**
pages 63, 65, 66, 69, 70, 74, 84 and 96

**Hint**

For this **discuss** question, you need to write about different ways service providers can work to make sure they deliver services that enable Beth to get the most out of them, given her mental ill health.

**Hint**

In your answer to this **discuss** question, you not only need to show that you have considered the service providers' various responsibilities but also include detail about each one.

**Watch out!**

Make sure you tie your answers into Beth's mental health issues, rather than just talking in general terms about the responsibilities of people who work in health and social care settings.

**Hint**

Use the number of marks available to guide your answer and how many points you should make to gain a high mark.

(d) Discuss how those who provide services for Beth can enable her to access, and benefit from, their services to meet her specific mental health needs.

........................................................................................................

........................................................................................................

........................................................................................................

........................................................................................................

........................................................................................................

........................................................................................................

........................................................................................................

........................................................................................................

........................................................................................................

........................................................................................................

........................................................................................................

........................................................................................................

........................................................................................................

........................................................................................................

........................................................................................................

**8 marks**

**Total for Question 1 = 20 marks**

# SECTION B

## Scenario 2: Learning disability

Joe is 33 years old and has learning difficulties. He lives in a residential care unit and works in a local supermarket. He really enjoys the independence he feels on leaving the unit, but he finds it hard to cope when school children make rude comments about him. He has talked to his social worker about this, who is concerned that Joe may lose his temper one day, which could lead to him losing his job.

Joe's family do not come and visit him very often, as they live some distance away. They also find it hard to cope with their guilt about not being able to care for him themselves, and their feelings of resentment at the cost of his care. He has lived in the unit for 10 years.

(a) Identify **two** ways in which Joe's social worker can support Joe, so he doesn't lose his job and, as a result of this, his limited independence.

1 ...................................................................................................................
...................................................................................................................

2 ...................................................................................................................
...................................................................................................................

2 marks

**Revision Guide**
pages 58, 59 and 97

**Hint**

For this **identify** question, you simply need to state two ways in which the social worker can support Joe in this situation. You don't need to add any detail.

**Hint**

Keep the answers to **identify** questions concise and specific. Don't waste time writing lots of points for which you won't gain any marks, as you will need that time when you are answering the longer questions.

**Hint**

Firstly, think about what Joe's social worker could suggest, and to whom, at the supermarket. Secondly, consider whether there is any training or counselling that can be arranged to help Joe.

**Revision Guide**
pages 64
and 86

**Hint**

For this **describe** question, you need to state two ways in which services can adapt their service provision – and you also need to add some detail to say how each one helps the service user who has learning disabilities.

**Hint**

Your answer can be about how the service provider behaves towards people with learning difficulties **and** how the service provider protects them from other service users' negativity.

**Hint**

Think about how you might feel if you were a GP's receptionist and Joe was struggling to explain to you exactly what he wanted. In the meantime, some of the people queuing behind him were showing their irritation at being kept waiting. What should you do in this situation?

(b) Describe **two** ways in which health and social care services can adapt their provision for people with learning difficulties like Joe.

1 ...................................................................................................................

...................................................................................................................

...................................................................................................................

...................................................................................................................

2 ...................................................................................................................

...................................................................................................................

...................................................................................................................

...................................................................................................................

4 marks

(c) Explain how Joe will probably have been assessed before being given a place at the residential care unit.

..................................................................................................................

..................................................................................................................

..................................................................................................................

..................................................................................................................

..................................................................................................................

..................................................................................................................

..................................................................................................................

..................................................................................................................

..................................................................................................................

..................................................................................................................

6 marks

**Revision Guide**
page 83

**Hint**

For this **explain** question, you need to explain what the assessor was looking at, and the questions they will have asked, when they visited Joe to carry out the assessment.

**Hint**

The number of marks available will give you a good guideline for how many valid points you should make to gain a high mark.

**Hint**

Don't forget to mention that adult social services will carry out the assessment, as this is an important part of showing that you understand how Joe will have been assessed.

**Revision Guide**
page 59

## Prepare

If you have time, make a plan by noting down two sets of bullet points, listing the advantages and disadvantages of residential care for Joe. You can tick them off as you write your answer – then you can be sure you have covered everything you want to include.

## Hint

Use the number of marks available to guide your answer and the number of advantages and disadvantages you should write about. Try to include a good balance of each to gain a high mark.

## Hint

Remember that the advantages and disadvantages can be about both Joe and his parents.

## Hint

When answering a **discuss** question, you need to connect the points you make so that your answer is coherent and makes sense.

(d) Discuss the advantages and disadvantages of Joe being in residential care.

..................................................................................................................

..................................................................................................................

..................................................................................................................

..................................................................................................................

..................................................................................................................

..................................................................................................................

..................................................................................................................

..................................................................................................................

..................................................................................................................

..................................................................................................................

..................................................................................................................

..................................................................................................................

..................................................................................................................

..................................................................................................................

**8 marks**

**Total for Question 2 = 20 marks**

# SECTION C

**Revision Guide**
pages 62
and 98

### Scenario 3: Physical/sensory disability

Branwen is 52 years old and has recently become a wheelchair user after a fall from a horse left her paralysed from the waist down. She lives at home with her husband, Dylan. They have a large home in the country with stables to house their horses.

She is happy to be home after over a year in hospital, followed by time in a rehabilitation unit. Since her accident she has been supported by a team of health and social care professionals such as paramedics, physiotherapists, occupational therapists and social workers. She is hoping to return to her job soon, working in the office of a local high school, as she misses seeing her friends and colleagues. Branwen feels that by returning to work, her life will have more purpose and she will regain more of her independence.

(a) Identify **two** practical ways in which social services will have supported Branwen to enable her to leave the rehabilitation unit and return home.

1 ................................................................................................................................

................................................................................................................................

2 ................................................................................................................................

................................................................................................................................

**2 marks**

**Hint**

The command word in this question is **identify**, so you only need to state the two facts asked for, without adding any detail.

**Hint**

Think about what you would need to change in your home if you had an accident and had to use a wheelchair.

**Watch out!**

This question asks about practical ways social services will have supported Branwen's move back to her home, which means physical rather than emotional support.

Revision Guide
page 82

**Hint**

This is a **describe** question, so you need to add more detail than you would for an identify question.

**Hint**

Try to include at least two relevant points, with a brief description of why each is good, to gain a high mark.

**Hint**

Think about how you would feel and what might happen if you were forced to live away from home for any length of time.

**LEARN IT!**

Care at home is called **domiciliary care**.

(b) Describe why a high proportion of care takes place at home rather than in residential care.

.................................................................................................................

.................................................................................................................

.................................................................................................................

.................................................................................................................

.................................................................................................................

.................................................................................................................

.................................................................................................................

**4 marks**

(c) Explain the responsibilities of health and social care professionals who help Branwen continue to stay healthy and to live as independently as possible.

..................................................................................................................

..................................................................................................................

..................................................................................................................

..................................................................................................................

..................................................................................................................

..................................................................................................................

..................................................................................................................

..................................................................................................................

..................................................................................................................

..................................................................................................................

6 marks

**Revision Guide**
pages 62
and 82

**Hint**

For this **explain** question, you need to identify some responsibilities and expand on each one to include some detail.

**Hint**

As this question is worth 6 marks, you should try to identify three responsibilities and add at least one piece of detail to each.

**Explore**

In this scenario, another consideration might be the type of formal support Branwen and Dylan may need as they become older and Dylan is less able to help Branwen.

**Revision Guide**
page 91

**Revision Guide** page 91

**Hint**

For this **discuss** question, you need to state what aspects of regulation are covered by the HCPC and add some detail for each.

**Hint**

Remember that this question is worth 8 marks. Use this knowledge to guide your answer and the number of relevant points you make, aiming to demonstrate that your knowledge is accurate and thorough.

**Hint**

To structure this answer you need to write about:

- registration
- the different standards set by the HCPC
- what they promote
- what they protect the public from
- what they investigate.

**Watch out!**

This is a general question about professionals who provide services for people like Branwen, so you don't need to relate your answer specifically to Branwen.

(d) Discuss how professionals such as paramedics, physiotherapists, occupational therapists and social workers are regulated by the Health and Care Professions Council (HCPC).

......................................................................................................................

......................................................................................................................

......................................................................................................................

......................................................................................................................

......................................................................................................................

......................................................................................................................

......................................................................................................................

......................................................................................................................

......................................................................................................................

......................................................................................................................

......................................................................................................................

......................................................................................................................

......................................................................................................................

......................................................................................................................

8 marks

Total for Question 3 = 20 marks

# SECTION D

**Revision Guide** pages 56 and 60

**Scenario 4: Age-related needs (early childhood)**

Lavelle is two months old. His mother Angelique went into labour eight weeks early while Angelique and Jean-Claude, her husband, were on holiday in England. She felt very supported by her midwife, Sarah, both during and after the birth.

Lavelle choked and stopped breathing while he was still in hospital. A doctor resuscitated him on the spot. He was then taken to theatre for surgery after a scan showed he had been born with a blockage in his intestine. He was in hospital for six weeks, and his parents visited him twice a day, every day, in the neonatal care unit where they were able to feed him using a syringe.

You met Lavelle and his parents a few weeks ago when you were sent to observe on the unit as a trainee nurse.

(a) Identify **two** roles carried out by midwives.

1 ...........................................................................................................

...........................................................................................................

2 ...........................................................................................................

...........................................................................................................

**2 marks**

**Hint**

The command word in this question is **identify** so you only need to state the facts asked for.

**Hint**

The obvious answer is 'to deliver babies'. If you can't remember another role of a midwife, think about when you have seen babies being born on television in medical dramas or soaps.

**LEARN IT!**

**Antenatal care** is care provided before the birth of the baby.

**Postnatal care** is provided after the birth.

**Neonatal care** is the type of care a baby born premature or sick receives in a neonatal unit.

**Revision Guide**
pages 56, 60
and 95

### Hint

For this **describe** question, you need to include some detail about each point you make. So, after each skill you identify, add detail, such as an example of using that skill or why it is needed.

### Watch out!

This question is about you as a trainee nurse, not Sarah as a midwife. It is also about skills not qualities, so you will not gain any marks for writing about qualities such as empathy and kindness.

### Hint

Answer the question as though you are the trainee nurse describing two professional skills you will need to learn. If you are asked a question which seems to be about you, remember to re-read the information provided in the scenario to remind yourself what your role is in the question.

(b) Describe **two** professional skills you will need to learn in order to work with a baby such as Lavelle.

1 ......................................................................................................................

......................................................................................................................

......................................................................................................................

......................................................................................................................

2 ......................................................................................................................

......................................................................................................................

......................................................................................................................

......................................................................................................................

4 marks

(c) Explain how following policies and procedures protects you as a trainee nurse when working in a hospital.

..............................................................................................................

..............................................................................................................

..............................................................................................................

..............................................................................................................

..............................................................................................................

..............................................................................................................

..............................................................................................................

..............................................................................................................

..............................................................................................................

..............................................................................................................

..............................................................................................................

..............................................................................................................

6 marks

**Revision Guide**
page 101

**Hint**

For this **explain** question, you need to identify ways in which policies and procedures protect you as a service provider **and** also add some detail for each example you write about.

**Hint**

Aim to explain at least three ways in which you are protected and include some detail for each in your answer to gain a good mark. If you can't think of much detail, include more ways, to show your understanding.

**LEARN IT!**

**Policies** comprise a service provider's statements of intent and a description of the procedures to be followed to ensure that codes of practice and regulations are adhered to.

**Procedures** are step-by-step instructions that employees must follow when completing a particular task to the standard required by their employer.

**Watch out!**

This question is about **you** being protected as a service provider, **not** how service users are protected. You will not gain any marks if you write about protecting service users.

**Revision Guide**
page 102

If you have time, before you start to write your answer list some key words to help keep your answer focused.

**Hint**

For this **discuss** question, you need to pick some of the principles and include some detail with each one.

**Hint**

The number of principles you should include in your answer will depend on how much detail you include. For example, you could identify four principles and expand each to include some detail.

**Hint**

If you cannot remember any specific nursing values, write about how you would behave as a nurse to empower service users (each nursing principle is based on the care values).

**Hint**

Remember to answer this question using the first person, i.e. 'I would...'.

(d) Discuss how you would follow the principles of nursing practice to provide safe and effective nursing care.

..............................................................................................................

..............................................................................................................

..............................................................................................................

..............................................................................................................

..............................................................................................................

..............................................................................................................

..............................................................................................................

..............................................................................................................

..............................................................................................................

..............................................................................................................

..............................................................................................................

..............................................................................................................

..............................................................................................................

..............................................................................................................

..............................................................................................................

8 marks

Total for Question 4 = 20 marks

**TOTAL FOR PAPER = 80 MARKS**

# Practice assessment 4

## SECTION A

> **Answer ALL questions.**
> **Write your answers in the spaces provided.**

**1**

### Scenario 1: Ill health

Malik is 15 years old and was born with cystic fibrosis. This means he has a daily build-up of thick sticky mucus in his lungs, digestive system and other organs, so his whole body is affected. He has reduced lung function and spends hours every day having physiotherapy and taking nebulised treatments, as well as tablets to help him digest his food.

His parents have always cared for him at home, with frequent stays in hospital, but, after a series of infections, he is now very ill. He is receiving palliative care in a hospice, which is close to his home. The hospice is run by a charity, which means it is in the voluntary or third sector. His main nurse is called Julie.

(a) Identify **two** ways in which Julie will help and support Malik and his family.

1  .................................................................................................................

   .................................................................................................................

2  .................................................................................................................

   .................................................................................................................

> **2 marks**

**Revision Guide**
page 80

## Time it!

Time yourself completing this practice assessment. You should try to do it within 90 minutes. Details of the timing for the actual assessment may change so check the latest guidance on the Pearson website to make sure you are up to date.

### Hint

For this **identify** question, you only need to provide the facts asked for, with no added detail.

### Hint

This question asks about both Malik **and** his family.

### LEARN IT!

**Palliative care** is offered to people towards the end of their lives and is sometimes called end-of-life care.

**Revision Guide**
pages 73, 74
and 80

### Hint

This is a **describe** question, so you need to identify two features of palliative care and add some detail about each of them.

### Hint

To answer this question think about what services might be offered to someone in Malik's situation and their family, and how these will work together. Imagine what the hospice staff would aim to do for Malik and his family, as he is dying.

### Watch out!

The question is asking for characteristics of palliative care in general, so think about how to describe palliative care rather than the healthcare offered to someone who is ill but who will recover. This question is not about the roles of staff in the hospice.

(b) Describe **two** characteristics of palliative care.

1 .......................................................................................................................

.......................................................................................................................

.......................................................................................................................

.......................................................................................................................

2 .......................................................................................................................

.......................................................................................................................

.......................................................................................................................

.......................................................................................................................

**4 marks**

(c) Explain the key features of a voluntary organisation such as a hospice.

..............................................................................................................................

..............................................................................................................................

..............................................................................................................................

..............................................................................................................................

..............................................................................................................................

..............................................................................................................................

..............................................................................................................................

..............................................................................................................................

..............................................................................................................................

..............................................................................................................................

..............................................................................................................................

..............................................................................................................................

**6 marks**

**Revision Guide**
pages 78 and 85

**Hint**

For this **explain** question, you need to include some detail in your answers.

**Hint**

Be guided by the number of marks available – aim to identify three features and write at least one detail about each. For example, one answer could be 'non-profit making' and the added detail should explain what the hospice might do with any surplus income.

**Hint**

The question asks about key features, which means you need to write about what makes a voluntary organisation different from a public or private sector organisation.

**Revision Guide**
pages 71, 91
and 102

**Hint**

For this **discuss** question, you need to show that you have considered the various ways in which nurses are regulated and include detail about each one.

**Hint**

Remember that you need to write about both **why** nurses are regulated as well as **how** they are regulated by external organisations.

**Hint**

Use the number of marks available to guide how many points you make in your answer. It is good to show that you know about at least two external organisations which regulate nurses.

**LEARN IT!**

**Regulations** set the standards of professional conduct required of people who work in health and social care settings. Regulations must be followed by law.

**Watch out!**

You are being asked about how nurses are **regulated** so if you include any details about inspection you will not gain any extra marks.

(d) Discuss why and how nurses such as Julie are regulated by external organisations.

....................................................................................................

....................................................................................................

....................................................................................................

....................................................................................................

....................................................................................................

....................................................................................................

....................................................................................................

....................................................................................................

....................................................................................................

....................................................................................................

....................................................................................................

....................................................................................................

....................................................................................................

....................................................................................................

8 marks

Total for Question 1 = 20 marks

# SECTION B

**Answer ALL questions.
Write your answers in the spaces provided.**

**Revision Guide**
pages 58, 86
and 97

**2**

**Scenario 2: Learning disability**

Chrissie is 26 years old and has learning difficulties. She lives in a flat in the community and has a support worker, Emma, who helps her with day-to-day living.

Although she receives benefits and has enough to live on, Chrissie wants to get a job so she can meet people. Emma has just helped her to get a voluntary job in a local charity shop. Chrissie is worried about how people will react to her because people have said unkind things to her when she has been shopping locally.

(a) Identify **two** ways in which Emma may have helped Chrissie get the job.

1 ....................................................................................................................

....................................................................................................................

2 ....................................................................................................................

....................................................................................................................

2 marks

**Hint**

For this **identify** question, you simply need to state two ways in which Emma is likely to have supported Chrissie in this situation, without adding any detail.

**Hint**

First think about what you would need to do when applying for a job. What would someone with learning difficulties struggle with?

**Hint**

Remember that Emma is a support worker not a social worker, so she will help Chrissie with the practicalities of day-to-day life, including applying for a job.

**Revision Guide**
pages 58, 69
and 70

## Hint

As the command word is **describe** you need to not only state two ways in which Emma will protect Chrissie's personal data but also add some detail about each.

## Hint

Emma has to keep Chrissie's personal data secure but there will be times when she needs to share it with others. Think about who and why.

## Hint

Think about all the places where information about you is recorded and stored. Remember that data includes photos as well as written records.

## ⏱ Time it!

This **describe** question is worth 4 marks so don't use too much time by writing more than you need to. Aim to spend no more than four minutes writing and then checking your answer.

---

(b) Describe **two** ways in which Emma should protect data about Chrissie as required by the law.

1 ...........................................................................................

...........................................................................................

...........................................................................................

...........................................................................................

2 ...........................................................................................

...........................................................................................

...........................................................................................

...........................................................................................

4 marks

(c) Explain how Emma can help protect Chrissie from discrimination in the community.

....................................................................................................

....................................................................................................

....................................................................................................

....................................................................................................

....................................................................................................

....................................................................................................

....................................................................................................

....................................................................................................

....................................................................................................

....................................................................................................

....................................................................................................

6 marks

**Revision Guide**
pages 63, 64
and 86

**Hint**

For this **explain** question you need to state ways in which Emma can help Chrissie with this aspect of her life and add some detail about each one.

**Hint**

Be guided by the number of marks available – in this case you could write about three ways in which Emma can help protect Chrissie from discrimination and then add some detail about each of these ways.

**Hint**

The community includes services Chrissie needs, such as her GP, optician and dentist; her landlord; her neighbours; and the charity shop she is going to work in.

**Time it!**

Aim to spend no longer than six minutes on your answer, including time to read and check what you have written and amend it if necessary.

**Revision Guide**
pages 75, 92, 93, 94 and 101

**Hint**

For this **discuss** question, you need to consider a range of responsibilities Emma's employer has towards her.

**Prepare**

To ensure you write about enough responsibilities to gain high marks, you could write a bullet list before you start. Tick off each bullet once you've covered it in your answer.

**Time it!**

Try not to spend any longer than eight minutes answering this question.

**Explore**

Remember that policies, procedures, codes of practice and regulations exist to protect both the service user and the service provider, so in this case both Chrissie and Emma.

(d) Discuss the responsibilities which Emma's employer (the social services department) has towards her.

......................................................................................................................

......................................................................................................................

......................................................................................................................

......................................................................................................................

......................................................................................................................

......................................................................................................................

......................................................................................................................

......................................................................................................................

......................................................................................................................

......................................................................................................................

......................................................................................................................

......................................................................................................................

......................................................................................................................

......................................................................................................................

......................................................................................................................

8 marks

**Total for Question 2 = 20 marks**

# SECTION C

**Answer ALL questions.**
**Write your answers in the spaces provided.**

**Scenario 3: Physical disabilities**

Jasmine is five years old and has a syndrome which means she cannot walk. She also has health issues, although these are controlled with medication and operations. She uses a wheelchair, attends her local primary school and lives at home with her family. However, she often has to return to hospital for various procedures to improve her quality of life. She has a social worker, Rana, who supports her and her family, and a team of medical staff at the hospital who all know her.

(a) The Disclosure and Barring Service (DBS) carries out checks on all adults who want to work with children to make sure they are suitable to do so. Identify **two** facts they would check about any adult applying to work with children.

1  ........................................................................................................................

   ........................................................................................................................

2  ........................................................................................................................

   ........................................................................................................................

2 marks

**Revision Guide**
pages 67, 72 and 103

**Hint**

The command word in this question is **identify**, so you only need to state the two facts asked for, without adding any detail.

**Hint**

Think about what might be found in a person's background which would suggest that person is not suitable to work with children.

**Hint**

This is a general question which means you don't have to refer to Jasmine specifically in your answer.

**Explore**

The vetting of individuals who work with children or vulnerable adults was reviewed following the Bichard Report (2004) after the murders of Jessica Chapman and Holly Wells in 2002.

**Revision Guide**
page 72

**Hint**

This is a **describe** question, so you need to add more detail than if you were answering an identify question.

**Hint**

Try to include at least two relevant points and some detail about each to gain a good mark.

**Hint**

If you think you don't know anything specific about the work of a LSCB, write about what needs to be done to safeguard children by making sure safeguarding regulations are adhered to, and you will get some marks. This is better than leaving the question unanswered.

**Time it!**

Use the number of marks available to guide you on how much time to spend on this question. If you get a bit stuck, don't spend too long on it!

(b) Every local authority has a Local Safeguarding Children Board (LSCB). Describe the job of such a body in keeping children safe.

..................................................................................................................

..................................................................................................................

..................................................................................................................

..................................................................................................................

..................................................................................................................

..................................................................................................................

..................................................................................................................

4 marks

(c) Explain the performance criteria which should be demonstrated by those who work on the reception desk in Jasmine's hospital ward in order to meet the National Occupational Standards for receiving visitors.

.......................................................................................................................

.......................................................................................................................

.......................................................................................................................

.......................................................................................................................

.......................................................................................................................

.......................................................................................................................

.......................................................................................................................

.......................................................................................................................

.......................................................................................................................

.......................................................................................................................

.......................................................................................................................

.......................................................................................................................

**6 marks**

**Revision Guide**
*page 92*

**Hint**

As the command word in this question is **explain**, you need to identify some performance criteria of the National Occupational Standards for receiving visitors and add some detail as to how these can be met.

**Hint**

This question is worth 6 marks, so you could identify three performance criteria and add at least one piece of detail to each.

**Hint**

Think about how you would like to be treated by a nurse or volunteer working on a reception desk if you were going to visit a relative or close friend in hospital.

**LEARN IT!**

The **National Occupational Standards** (NOS) are statements of standards of performance, knowledge and understanding which individuals must achieve when carrying out specific tasks in the workplace.

**Revision Guide**
pages 73, 74, 95, 98 and 99

## Hint

As this is a **discuss** question you need to state various aspects of their combined role and add some detail to show how each aspect helps Jasmine stay healthy and independent. For example, you could say that professionals would help Jasmine's parents access other services (for example, obtaining equipment to help Jasmine be more independent).

## Hint

Use the number of marks available to guide your answer and how many points you need to make to demonstrate that your knowledge is accurate and thorough. For example, you could identify four different aspects of the professionals' role and add detail about each.

## Hint

Remember that this question is about the **overall role** of all the various health and social care professionals who look after Jasmine, such as her social worker and the team at her local hospital.

## Time it!

Don't forget that you only have 90 minutes to complete this paper. This question should take you a maximum of eight minutes. Remember to spend part of that time reading through your answer to check you haven't made any mistakes.

(d) Discuss the role of health and social care professionals in helping Jasmine continue to stay as healthy and independent as possible.

......................................................................................................................................

......................................................................................................................................

......................................................................................................................................

......................................................................................................................................

......................................................................................................................................

......................................................................................................................................

......................................................................................................................................

......................................................................................................................................

......................................................................................................................................

......................................................................................................................................

......................................................................................................................................

......................................................................................................................................

......................................................................................................................................

......................................................................................................................................

8 marks

Total for Question 3 = 20 marks

# SECTION D

> **Answer ALL questions.**
> **Write your answers in the spaces provided.**

**Revision Guide**
page 100

**4**

---

**Scenario 4: Age-related needs (later adulthood)**

Bill is 78 years old and lives in a residential care home. Although he is physically frail and needs help with his mobility, he is very alert and joins in with the activities arranged by the activities officer at the home. He enjoys board games, quizzes and trips out in the minibus accompanied by a care assistant.

You are the manager of the home and enjoy spending time with the residents when time allows, including Bill because he is interesting: he likes to talk about his early childhood at the end of the Second World War, his old friends and his family life. You overhear the activities officer commenting that Bill is boring and that she doesn't intend to give him a place on the minibus on the next trip. You tell her that this is not acceptable. She looks embarrassed and says she was only joking.

---

(a) Identify **two** of Bill's rights as a resident of the care home.

1 ...................................................................................................................

...................................................................................................................

2 ...................................................................................................................

...................................................................................................................

**2 marks**

**Hint**

The command word in this question is **identify** so you only need to state the facts asked for.

**Hint**

Think about what the activities officer said. Is this fair? Is Bill being treated equally? Is he being allowed to express a preference or to have a choice? This will give you some ideas as to some of his rights.

**Revision Guide**
pages 71, 76, 88, 89, 90 and 91

### Hint

For this **describe** question, you need to include some detail about each point you make.

### Hint

Remember to answer the question as though you are the manager of the care home, for example, 'I have to...'.

### Watch out!

This question is about you as the manager of a care home so is about social care, not healthcare. This means you will not gain marks for writing about any healthcare professional bodies.

### Watch out!

If you refer to specific professional bodies, be sure that they are UK ones and that you are using the correct name.

(b) Describe **two** ways in which you as a manager are accountable to professional bodies.

1 .........................................................................................................................

.........................................................................................................................

.........................................................................................................................

.........................................................................................................................

2 .........................................................................................................................

.........................................................................................................................

.........................................................................................................................

.........................................................................................................................

4 marks

(c) Explain how the local authority will have used needs assessment to check if Bill met the eligibility criteria for personal care to give him a place in the care home.

......................................................................................................................................

......................................................................................................................................

......................................................................................................................................

......................................................................................................................................

......................................................................................................................................

......................................................................................................................................

......................................................................................................................................

......................................................................................................................................

......................................................................................................................................

......................................................................................................................................

......................................................................................................................................

6 marks

**Revision Guide**
*page 83*

**Hint**

To answer this **explain** question you need to show that you know and understand the three eligibility criteria and, also, that you know that Bill needed to meet all three to be given his place in the care home.

**Hint**

To gain a good mark, you need to state each of the three eligibility criteria, and, when you write about the criterion involving specified outcomes, include some examples. You also need to say that Bill met all three criteria and explain why.

**Hint**

To find out why Bill matched all three eligibility criteria, re-read the scenario information at the start of question 4 (see page 61).

**Revision Guide**
pages 58, 66, 67, 68, 75 and 100

### Hint

For this **discuss** question, you need to pick some ways that you would encourage care assistants to keep Bill active and mobile as long as possible, and include some detail about each one.

### Hint

The number of ways you need to include in your answer to gain a good mark will depend on how much detail you include. You could identify four ways and expand each to include some detail, to show you have considered a range of ways.

### Hint

Don't forget to write your answer as if you are the care manager, for example 'I would...'.

### Watch out!

This question is about keeping Bill as active and mobile as possible, so writing about any other responsibilities, such as keeping Bill's personal data confidential, will not gain you any marks.

 **Time it!**

Remember that you have about eight minutes to complete this part of the question. Within this timeframe, try to leave a little time for checking what you have written (to make sure you have made enough relevant points and detail to gain a good mark).

(d) Discuss how you would support your care assistants to follow procedures to keep Bill as active and mobile as possible, for as long as possible.

......................................................................................................

......................................................................................................

......................................................................................................

......................................................................................................

......................................................................................................

......................................................................................................

......................................................................................................

......................................................................................................

......................................................................................................

......................................................................................................

......................................................................................................

......................................................................................................

......................................................................................................

......................................................................................................

**8 marks**

Total for Question 4 = 20 marks

**TOTAL FOR PAPER = 80 MARKS**

# Answers

The questions and sample answers are provided to help you revise content and develop your skills. Ask your tutor or check the Pearson website for the most up-to-date Sample Assessment Material, past papers and mark schemes to get an indication of the actual exam and what this requires of you. Details of the actual exam may change so always make sure you are up to date.

Use this section to check your answers. Note that answers to questions are individual and some may require longer responses; bullet points show the key points you could include in your answer or how your answer could be structured. For these questions, your answers should be written using sentences and paragraphs and you might include some, but not necessarily all of the points.

## Practice assessment 1

### (pages 1 to 16)

For all the questions, use the number of marks available to guide your answers and the number of points you should make to gain a high mark.

1  (a) Example content may include:
   • Help him access the healthcare services he needs.
   • Arrange for any adaptations needed in his home to enable him to cope with day-to-day tasks.
   • Help with access to benefits.
   • Help him cope as he adjusts to normal living away from the hospital.
   • Support his family and friends.
   • Ensure that his care reflects his needs and preferences.

   (b) Example content may include:
   • Empower him by supporting him and making sure he is not discriminated against due to his disability, making sure he has access to all the services he needs.
   • Empower him by finding ways to help him that allow him to keep his dignity, such as providing a grabber, so he can pick things up himself instead of relying on others.
   • Empower him by finding ways and equipment to help him be as independent as possible.
   • Empower him by making sure his care reflects his choices and promotes his wellbeing.
   • Empower him by promoting his rights, such as making sure he knows how to complain if he feels his needs are not being met.
   • Make sure he is safe by arranging for adaptations to be made so any risk is minimised, such as grab rails in the shower on his left-hand side as his right arm does not work.
   • Make sure he is safe by ensuring that another qualified support worker is on call to help if Tama is not available.
   • Maintain confidentiality by only sharing information about him and his condition with those who are involved in his care.

   (c) Example content may include:
   • An occupational therapist can visit Nigel at home to identify issues he has in everyday life, such as cooking.
   • The occupational therapist can help him work out practical solutions, such as having a small vacuum cleaner both upstairs and downstairs as he struggles to lift items like this.
   • His GP can provide prescriptions, so he can continue his medication without returning to the hospital.
   • His consultant at the hospital will continue to see him regularly to check on his progress and his brain injury.

   • A physiotherapist will work with Nigel regularly to help him maintain and, hopefully, improve his mobility.
   • A psychologist can help him cope with his anxiety and depression caused by his condition, and help improve his quality of life.

   (d) Example content may include:
   • Provides policies, procedures and codes of practice to follow.
   • Ensures policies, procedures and codes of practice are regularly reviewed and updated to make sure they support current national work practices, policies and legislation.
   • Is available to advise the support worker if she needs any help.
   • Provides any records/details she needs before starting to work with Nigel.
   • Monitors the support worker to make sure the service she provides meets National Occupational Standards (NOS).
   • Provides opportunities for continuing professional development (CPD).
   • Provides a complaints procedure for the service user and the support worker.
   • Ensures any complaints are dealt with properly.
   • Encourages the support worker to have membership of a trade union/professional association.
   • Provides a whistleblowing policy which protects the support worker if she feels the workplace practices that she is expected to implement are unsafe.

2  (a) Example content may include:
   How to:
   • use public transport
   • manage money
   • shop
   • do household tasks
   • cook safely
   • look after his personal hygiene.

   (b) Example content may include:
   • The need to make sure that Owen and his family have a say in his care, which means the day centre needs to offer a range of options to give them choices.
   • The conflict between trying to preserve Owen's independence and the obligation to report risk if they suspect there is any.
   • Owen is a strong and fit 22-year-old male, so if he loses his temper it may be hard for some staff to deal with him.
   • Providing care that is individualised enough for Owen when they have other service users with different needs.

   (c) Example content may include:
   Attending meetings with Owen or completing paperwork on his behalf in order to help him to:
   • express his views and opinions about his care and needs, so they are taken seriously
   • access information and services
   • defend and promote his rights and responsibilities
   • explore his choices and options.

   (d) Example content may include:
   • Ensure that they have a robust health and safety policy and that there is someone identified as being responsible for health and safety.
   • Undertake a risk assessment to identify risks and hazards and take action to reduce the likelihood of harm or injury.
   • Provide health and safety training for all staff and volunteers.
   • Keep a record of all accidents and incidents.

- Have a robust safeguarding policy.
- Protect from illness by, for example, having clean toilets, hand-washing facilities and safe drinking water.
- Provide well-maintained first aid facilities.
- Use protective equipment and clothing, for example, when dealing with any body fluids.
- Control substances harmful to health, such as cleaning fluids, by keeping them in a locked steel cupboard.
- Have enough staff to be able to adequately care for all service users.
- Make sure all staff have Disclosure and Barring Service (DBS) clearance.
- Ensure they have codes of practice which are familiar to, and followed by, all staff.
- Ensure that all staff have knowledge of infection control procedures.

**3** (a) Example content may include:
- Help her learn to do day-to-day tasks without her sight.
- Arrange adaptations to her home.
- Advise on appliances and other specialist aids available.
- Provide emotional support.
- Arrange for her to access other services, such as a psychologist or an occupational therapist, to help her adapt to her new circumstances.
- Provide information and support for her family and friends.
- Provide links for support groups.

(b) Example content may include:
- Make sure information transferred electronically is either encrypted or password protected.
- Make sure any written records are stored in a locked filing cabinet.
- Adhere to codes of practice regarding confidentiality provided by the social worker's employers.
- Only share information with others directly involved in Angie's care.
- Follow the policy provided by her employer on the use of mobile phones.

(c) Example content may include:
- She cannot see to use the phone to make the appointment.
- She will need someone to be available to go with her, to escort or take her to the appointment and to help her while there.
- There may be steps up to the front door which Angie will find harder to climb up as she can't see them, even with someone holding her arm.
- Angie will not be able to read any directions or other printed information when she gets there.
- There may be signs in Braille, but until she can read this fluently they will not help.
- Angie will not be able to complete any forms and will have to rely on the person with her, or the service provider, to do this for her.

(d) Example content may include:
- The Care Quality Commission (CQC):
  o registers care providers
  o monitors, inspects and rates services
  o takes action to protect service users if necessary
  o publishes inspection reports.
- The National Institute for Health and Care Excellence (NICE):
  o produces evidence-based guidance and advice for service providers
  o develops quality standards and performance measures for service providers
  o provides a range of information services
  o advises on the safety and effectiveness of services.
- The Health and Care Professional Council (HCPC):
  o promotes good practice

o protects the public from poor standards of care
o registers members of professions such as social workers
o investigates complaints and takes appropriate action.

**4** (a) Example content may include:
- To be treated fairly and equally.
- To be consulted about her care.
- To be consulted about her preferences, such as what to eat or wear, or when to pray.
- To be protected from risk or harm.
- To have access to the complaints procedures.

(b) Example content may include:
Line manager will:
- watch me carry out various procedures, such as changing a dressing, so she or he can tell me how to improve if necessary
- provide me with opportunities for training courses or continuous professional development (CPD), so I can learn, use and improve my skills
- make sure I have access to, and have read, all relevant documents that explain procedures that I need to be able to carry out
- check on skills, such as my record keeping, to make sure I don't need more training and to make suggestions for any improvements
- chat to service users as part of my performance management to gather feedback on the care I provide.

(c) Example content may include:
Under supervision by my line manager or other trained staff who are working near me I perform the following tasks:
- washing, dressing, toileting, making beds, feeding and helping service users with mobility
- monitoring health by taking readings such as temperature, pulse, respiration rate, blood pressure, oxygen level and weight
- providing correct information when answering questions from service users, their families and others involved in their care
- making sure notes are accurate and up to date
- following healthcare plans for each service user
- talking to service users, to give them company, keep their spirits up, reassure and comfort them
- keeping service users safe, for example, when they are using a walker reminding them not to sit down until the backs of their legs are touching the edge of their chair
- making sure I return records to their allocated place, so they are secure.

(d) Example content may include:
- All service providers work together so there is no need to keep repeating the details of Shama's case.
- Shama's different needs can be more easily assessed by multidisciplinary working.
- Gaps in provision can be identified and addressed.
- More efficient use of services, for example, a member of her family will be her primary carer when she returns home and a different service will assess that carer.
- Healthcare planning can be shared by all, so information is readily available and there is no break in Shama's care as she moves from hospital to the nursing home and then back home.
- Information sharing between professionals is more efficient.
- Care is provided in a coordinated way so services complement rather than disrupt each other, so less frustrating for all involved.
- Shama will feel she is being treated as a whole person, rather than having different services look after different parts of her care and not knowing what other services are doing.
- Shama and her family will be involved in the planning and decision-making about her care.
- A range of specialist services will be readily available to Shama and her family.

- Partnership working includes care planning cycle, monitoring and regular reviews, so Shama's care is constantly being updated to meet her current needs.
- Regular feedback on her care and progress empowers Shama and her family as it will feel that she is at the centre of the care rather than having the care 'being done' to her.

## Practice assessment 2

**(pages 17 to 32)**

For all the questions, use the number of marks available to guide your answers and the number of points you should make to gain a high mark.

**1** (a) Example content may include:
- Discuss Ava's treatment with them and ask for their opinion on various options.
- Explain exactly what is happening to Ava.
- Explain anything the family don't understand, such as some of the medical words or terms being used.
- Reassure and comfort them.

(b) Example content may include:
- Make sure all equipment is sterile, soiled dressings are disposed of properly and bedding is clean to reduce the risk of infection.
- Make sure she handles needles safely and disposes of sharps correctly after use.
- Make sure dosages are correct, so Ava doesn't receive too little or too much of a drug.
- Keep all drugs locked away until needed, so Ava doesn't take any by mistake.
- Take accurate medical notes and keep Ava's records updated, so the information is accurate.
- Keep Ava's records secure, so anyone not involved in her care can't access them.
- Follow the hospital's safeguarding policy/all relevant codes of conduct or policies, so she knows she is not increasing the risk of any harm to Ava by her own actions.
- Adhere to ward rules, such as visiting hours and numbers round a bed, making sure no stranger is able to approach Ava.
- Make sure that Ava has help eating when she is feeling poorly, has the correct diet and that her food isn't too hot.

(c) Example content may include:
- The doctors will provide medical care, treating and monitoring Ava's illness and liaising with other professionals, such as nurses and other specialist doctors, about her care.
- Her consultant/oncologist/specialist doctor will decide how her illness is treated and will liaise with other doctors to make sure the correct care is given.
- Healthcare assistants meet her care needs such as washing, toileting, changing her bed and helping her to eat.
- Cancer nurse specialists will administer and monitor treatment such as chemotherapy.
- Social workers will provide emotional support for both Ava and her family, and make sure all is as it should be at home before she is discharged.
- Radiologists may administer radiation therapy to target the cancer.
- Play specialists will make sure that Ava has activities that she can do and enjoy, making her stay in hospital more fun, helping her pass the time and ensuring that she is not missing out on playing.

(d) Example content may include:
- Gain qualifications by going to college and/or university.
- Undertake induction before starting their jobs.

- Undertake training while in post from other, more experienced, professionals working in the hospital.
- Undertake training while in post by accessing training provided by their regulatory bodies.
- Undertake continuing professional development throughout their careers, so their skills are maintained, improved and up to date.
- Read articles in professional journals.
- Keep up to date with changes in policies, regulations, procedures and codes of practice.
- Implement the National Occupational Standards (NOS).
- Adhere to the principles laid down by their professional bodies, such as the principles of nursing practice.

**2** (a) Example content may include:
- Lay down some strict boundaries with Janny and Rosie, in language they can both understand, making it clear that they are not allowed to be in private together until they know each other better, and tell them that the staff will be watching them carefully.
- Discourage Janny and Rosie from becoming intimate, explaining the possible consequences.
- Give advice on eventually having a safe, intimate relationship.

(b) Example content may include:
- Line manager allocates tasks to the support worker and monitors her work.
- Line manager gives her advice and helps her when she is unsure what to do.
- Line manager praises and encourages her if her work is of a high standard.
- If the support worker's performance falls short of the expected standard the line manager addresses the issues and takes appropriate action.

(c) Example content may include:
- Speak to the manager of the unit and other staff members to see if they have noticed anything wrong.
- The manager may suspend the support worker while the allegation is investigated.
- Speak to Janny, with his parents present as advocates, and record his version of events.
- Share the complaints procedure with his parents and ask his parents if they want to make a formal complaint.
- Explain to Janny that he has nothing to fear from speaking up as this is a serious allegation.
- Interview the support worker and ask for her account, starting by explaining what was overheard, what the complaint is, that the social worker has to follow up the complaint and that the support worker can have another colleague/union representative along for support if she wishes.
- Take appropriate action based on the outcome of the investigation. If abuse is proven this action may be dismissal and referral to the police.

To gain a good mark you need to include something about interviewing Janny with an appropriate adult present, interviewing the support worker, the possibility of discrimination, speaking to other colleagues, the complaints procedure and taking action.

(d) Your answer should include:
- Residential care settings are inspected by The Care Quality Commission (CQC) in England, the Care and Social Services Inspectorate Wales (CSSIW) in Wales, and the Regulation and Quality Improvement Agency (RQIA) in Northern Ireland (you should mention the one relevant to where you live).

67

- Identifies the scope and purpose of the investigation.
- Gathers views of service users and staff.
- Observes service delivery.
- Reviews records, documents and policies.
- Gives feedback at a meeting with the inspection team and senior staff.
- Rates the service and publishes findings.
- Takes action to improve services and protect service users where needed.

**3** (a) Example content may include:
- Provide emotional support via the charity's helpline.
- Provide practical support.
- Provide information.
- Provide access to face-to-face support services.
- Give legal advice such as how to claim compensation.
- Speak on his behalf (advocate).
- Help him access the services he needs.

(b) Example content may include:
- Advise on specialist equipment to assist with daily activities, such as devices to help him do up buttons with one hand.
- Advise on home adaptations, such as grab rails, so he can, for example, shower safely.
- Help him work out practical solutions by trying different methods of tackling a task to find the method that works best for him.
- Assist him in returning to work by assessing what adaptations will be needed to support him to do his job.
- Organise his attendance at rehabilitation groups.

(c) Example content may include:
- He will be less likely to have accidents due to his disability, so will feel less self-conscious and more confident in tackling tasks.
- He will feel more positive and less of a victim, so will be more able to ask for, and accept, help from his family and friends.
- He will feel enabled to contribute to family life again, and feel less of a burden, so preserving his dignity and promoting his independence.

(d) Example content may include:
- A holistic approach will take account of Taj's wider needs (intellectual, emotional and social as well as physical).
- Care will be more personalised, and he will feel as though his needs are being better understood.
- Other issues that contribute to his health issues, such as stress and poor self-esteem due to his facial scarring, limp and the loss of his arm, will be identified and addressed.
- Being viewed as a whole person and not a medical problem will make him feel more valued.
- He will not only have his physical problems addressed but will also be able to access services such as psychological help.
- His social needs will be looked at, so, for example, alternative ways to access sport might be suggested.
- Taj could be offered counselling to help him come to terms with his disabilities and help him with his relationships with his family and friends.
- As he becomes more positive he will become more determined to work on his physical fitness and try to reduce his limp.

**4** (a) Example content may include:
- Charles is unable to get out of bed unaided to go to the toilet, so he may wet the bed.
- He is likely to try to get out of bed on his own, risking more injuries due to his osteoporosis.

(b) Example content may include:
- I would report my concern immediately to the manager on the grounds that I believe Charles's safety is at risk and his dignity is being compromised. If I am unable to access the manager, I would report to the most senior member of staff.

- I would expect that my involvement in reporting my colleagues would be kept confidential for the sake of working relationships.
- I would expect the manager to be glad that I had alerted him or her to what could be a very serious situation.
- I would expect to be treated fairly and not as though I am a troublemaker.

> The number of marks available (in this case, four) should guide you as to how much information you would need to include in your answer to gain high marks.

(c) Example content may include:
- Employees have a right to be protected from abuse of any form, so they could ask to speak to their line manager and request that discussions take place to adopt a zero tolerance approach.
- They could complain to their line manager, in this case probably a senior care assistant, whose job it is to help them resolve any problems they are having in their working life.
- If they feel they are not being listened to, they could report their concerns to the manager of the care home.
- If necessary, they could put their complaint in writing, so following the complaints procedure.
- If they were not happy with the response they got from the manager they could ask their trade union representative to accompany them to a meeting with the manager.

(d) Example content may include:
I should:
- follow policies and procedures in place in the care home
- talk to the residents and reassure them
- enable rehabilitation of any who are injured
- provide equipment and adaptation as required to support the service users to be more independent, such as walkers and wheelchairs
- provide personal care, such as washing, dressing, feeding and toileting
- help them take part in leisure activities
- listen to and respect their preferences, such as what they want to wear or eat
- help maintain their dignity by, for example, being discreet if a service user has wet the bed
- support them on trips out
- make accurate and adequate records of the care I give, such as recording weight and noting down when I help them to the toilet
- maintain confidentiality, making sure information is only shared with those involved in a service user's care
- help them access services, such as the visiting hairdresser
- encourage them to remain as active as possible to maintain as much mobility as possible, for example, attend armchair exercise classes
- make sure they eat enough, so they remain healthy and keep their strength up
- keep them safe and out of harm by reducing any risk, for example, making sure rugs are flat on the floor and bathroom floors are dry
- make sure they take any drugs issued straight away
- refer any concerns I have to more senior staff, such as any deterioration in a service user's health and wellbeing
- report any incidents or accidents immediately to my line manager or another senior member of staff.

# Practice assessment 3

## pages 33 to 48)

For all the questions, use the number of marks available to guide your answers and the number of points you should make to gain a high mark.

**1** (a) Example content may include:
- Anxiety, trouble sleeping and mood changes are all symptoms of stress so they may have put Beth's symptoms down to stress due to exam pressures.
- They may have thought Beth's issues were due to hormones and changes in her body.
- Beth appears to be outgoing and confident so there didn't appear to be anything wrong.

(b) Example content may include:
- Look after her physical health, by keeping active and eating a healthy diet.
- Drink sensibly, as alcohol can heighten emotions and make depression worse.
- See family and friends regularly, so she has company and a distraction.
- Ask for help when needed, rather than keeping her feelings bottled up which will make her feel worse.
- Go on holiday; do something she is good at or something she enjoys; do something to help someone else, such as babysit a favourite nephew or niece; or take up a new hobby. All these will provide a distraction.

(c) Example content may include:
- Her GP:
  o diagnoses then monitors her condition
  o prescribes medication
  o gives her information about her condition
  o refers her to other services such as counselling.
- A counsellor:
  o listens to her
  o offers her strategies to cope with how she is feeling
  o puts her in touch with support groups and/or services.
- A support service, such as the charity Mind:
  o provides information and tips for everyday living
  o provides a confidential helpline and online community to talk to others with similar mental health issues.

(d) Example content may include:
- Empower her by allowing her to express her needs and preferences. For example, Beth might not want anyone beyond her immediate family to know that she has depression and OCD as she may be worried about what others will think of her and if it will affect her promotion chances. In this case, if Beth needs time off work, her GP may put something less specific on her sick note.
- Enable her to access services at a time that avoids her working hours, so she has the choice as to whether or not to tell her employer.
- Give her the time she needs to talk through her problems.
- Reduce her anxiety by allowing her to see a service provider of a gender of her choice.
- Make sure her personal information is kept confidential, so, for example, give Beth access to a receptionist where she cannot be overheard when booking an appointment with a counsellor.
- Set her targets, for example, rather than just suggest a counsellor, her GP could ask that she makes an appointment with the counsellor before her next appointment with the GP.
- Help her overcome barriers, such as not wanting to ask for help, by encouraging her to keep in touch. For example, by saying when next they want to see her, so that they can monitor her condition.

- If she is getting worse, refer her for more specialist help, maybe even admitting her to hospital.
- Take a holistic approach, for example, helping her get more sleep may help her depression.
- Undertake continuing professional development so their knowledge of mental health issues is up to date.

**2** (a) Example content may include:
- Talk to the manager of the supermarket to see if Joe's hours can be adjusted so he is on a break just before school starts and after school ends.
- Arrange assertiveness training for Joe.
- Arrange counselling for Joe to learn some coping strategies.

(b) Example content may include:
- Make sure staff address their own prejudices and adapt their behaviour to ensure that people like Joe feel welcomed and supported, for example, by being patient and not showing any irritation if it takes the person some time to explain what they need.
- Train staff so they understand the needs of someone with learning difficulties.
- Make sure any written information is available in a form which is accessible, for example, shorter words, fewer words, colourful and illustrated.
- Encourage the use of advocates, so the person with learning difficulties has someone with them to help them express themselves clearly.
- Challenge any other service users who are showing any signs of discrimination towards people with learning difficulties.

(c) Example content may include:
Adult social services would have assessed:
- his previous living situation and whether it was suitable for him
- whether he could look after his own needs
- his needs and how these impact on his care
- his likes and dislikes regarding personal care
- his interests and aspirations
- the needs of his family
- his financial resources.

(d) Example content may include:
The advantages are that:
- trained staff are available to meet Joe's needs
- his dignity is maintained with his family because they are not helping him with day-to-day living tasks
- there are staff and other residents, who have similar issues to Joe, around to keep him company, so he is less likely to feel isolated
- activities are available to stimulate and help meet his particular needs
- he may feel more independent than living at home with his family
- his family are reassured that he is getting the care he needs and will continue to do so if anything happens to them.
The disadvantages are that:
- he may be upset at leaving his own family and home
- he may feel isolated from friends and relatives
- the cost of the care may cause problems for his family
- Joe's parents feel guilty for not looking after him themselves.

**3** (a) Example content may include:
- Made sure Branwen's home was adapted so she has access to all the rooms she needs. For example, suggesting either the installation of a lift or stairlift, or the adaption of a room downstairs to become a bedroom.
- Made sure she has the equipment she needs, such as a hoist or a wheel-in bath or shower in the bathroom.
- Checked that facilities, such as electrical sockets, are within reach and at the correct height for a wheelchair user.

(b) Example content may include:
- People are with their families and all their belongings, so are happier.
- People at home are more independent than those who live in residential care, so are happier.
- They are less likely to catch illnesses at home as there are fewer people living there, so they are healthier.
- It costs less to care for someone in their own home.

(c) Example content may include:
- Monitor and reassess Branwen's disability and involve her in any planning for her future.
- Keep Branwen informed of any research or new methods that could help her regain some of her mobility.
- Ensure Dylan is coping with helping her with her care because, if he becomes unable to do so, other, more formal, arrangements will need to be put in place to enable her to continue to live at home.
- Alert her to support groups for people with disabilities such as hers, so she can talk to others in her situation.
- Ensure that any information needed by other services is passed on securely and only to those directly involved in her care.
- Continue to ensure that she has all the care and support she needs.
- Help her return to work by recommending adaptations than can be made and suggesting her employer provides disability awareness training for her co-workers, looking at any health and safety issues.
- Follow the policies and procedures laid down by their employers.

(d) Your answer should include:
- Registers professionals who meet their standards for training, professional skills, behaviour and health.
- Sets standards for health and social care professionals in:
  o conduct and ethics, so they meet the standards of professional practice
  o performance and efficiency, so they deliver quality care
  o character and health, so they meet the standard of personal behaviour required
  o education and training, so they have achieved the relevant qualifications and attended the required training.
- Promotes good practice, including sharing any updates in practice or techniques.
- Protects the public from poor standards of care.
- Investigates complaints and takes appropriate action.

4 (a) Example content may include:
- Monitor and examine pregnant women.
- Help families prepare for parenthood via antenatal classes.
- Carry out screening tests such as ultrasound scans.
- Assist during labour and supervise pain management.
- Deliver babies.
- Provide postnatal care.

(b) Example content may include:
I will need to learn how to:
- make observations and take accurate measurements, such as Lavelle's temperature, in order to monitor his health
- take samples for analysis, such as a blood sample, to make sure the levels of various substances in his blood are correct
- provide personal care, such as sponging him in his incubator
- correctly administer any drugs needed, check the dosage and record it on his chart
- communicate effectively with his parents, to make sure they understand his care
- record all observations and measurements accurately on his chart.

(c) Example content may include:
When I follow policies and procedures I am protected because I am:
- implementing best practice to meet the needs of service users
- using the relevant skills required to work as a nurse
- working effectively with my colleagues
- adhering to guidelines that are designed to keep me safe at work
- minimising risk to myself
- more protected if anything goes wrong
- making appropriate, timely, professional and ethical responses
- making decisions and taking actions that are in line with current active legislation, so I am working within the law.

(d) Example content may include:
I would:
- treat everyone in my care with dignity, respect and humanity, showing I understand their individual needs
- take responsibility for the care I provide, and answer for my own actions and judgements
- manage and be vigilant about risk, and help keep everyone safe
- put people at the centre of their care, helping them make informed choices about their treatment and care
- make sure I communicate effectively by assessing, recording and reporting treatment, care and concerns, and handle information sensitively and confidentially
- keep my knowledge and skills up to date, and use them as well as I can to meet the needs of individuals
- work closely with others in my team and other professionals, so that patient care is coordinated, of high standard and has the best possible outcomes
- lead by example, being open and responding to individual needs.

## Practice assessment 4

**(pages 49 to 64)**

> For all the questions, use the number of marks available to guide your answers and the number of points you should make to gain a high mark.

1 (a) Example content may include:
- Take care of Malik's physical needs such as medication.
- Take care of Malik's intellectual needs, for example, by providing him with books and/or DVDs.
- Take care of Malik's emotional needs, for example, by comforting him.
- Take care of Malik's social needs, for example, by chatting to him.
- Control Malik's symptoms, so he is as comfortable as possible.
- Support Malik's family.

(b) Example content may include:
- Multidisciplinary, where all services work in partnership with the service user and family and friends.
- Holistic, so seeks to meet physical, intellectual, emotional and social needs.
- Manages pain and other symptoms rather than trying to cure the illness.

(c) Example content may include:
- Non-profit making so any surplus income is used to develop the hospice's services.
- Has paid staff as well as volunteers for some of their services, so will have volunteers who visit patients or who raise funds for the hospice, for example.

- Managed independently of central government or local authorities, providing services alongside those provided by public and private sector organisations.
- Funded by donations.

(d) Example content may include:

Why?
- To ensure they maintain high standards.
- To ensure they provide safe care.

How?
- Nurses must respond to regulations by making changes to their working practices where required and improving the services they offer. They are regulated by organisations such as:
- The Nursing and Midwifery Council:
  o ensures nurses in the UK have the right qualifications and skills
  o sets standards of practice and behaviour
  o requires nurses to challenge discrimination
  o requires nurses to review their own practice annually.
- The Royal College of Nursing:
  o sets out the principles of nursing practice, and nurses' roles and responsibilities in safeguarding
  o ensures accountability of nurses, promoting continuing professional development (CPD)
  o supports diversity in nursing.

**2** (a) Example content may include:
- Helped Chrissie complete an application form or write a CV.
- Helped her decide what to wear for the interview.
- Advised Chrissie, or supported her to have a practice run, thinking about what time to leave her flat and how to get there.
- Gone with her to the interview.
- Spoken on Chrissie's behalf or acted as her advocate when Chrissie was unsure.

(b) Example content may include:
- Make sure Chrissie's personal data is not kept on her own personal mobile phone, because the phone may get lost and then the data may be accessed by others.
- Not share any information about Chrissie with anyone not involved in her care, unless Chrissie gives her permission. Emma might share information in order to help Chrissie live as independently as possible, for example, when helping her to get a job. In an instance like this she would only supply basic information such as Chrissie's name, address, date of birth and particular needs relating to the workplace.
- Store any records she makes of the care and support she gives Chrissie securely, for example, in an encrypted file on a tablet, or locked away if a paper record.
- Not share any photos of Emma on social media, making sure that photos are only used for specific purposes such as recording her needs.

(c) Example content may include:
- Explain Chrissie's needs to the manager of the charity shop so the manager can monitor Chrissie's interactions with customers and step in if anyone shows any sign of discrimination against her.
- Explain Chrissie's needs to her landlord and neighbours, so they understand and know not to make any unkind remarks, and hopefully offer help and support.
- Challenge any policies the charity shop has that discriminate against people with learning disabilities.
- Challenge any service Chrissie uses that does not have information in a form that is easily accessible to people with learning difficulties. For example, her landlord, GP, optician, dentist or the charity shop, who may all provide information.
- Make sure longer appointment times are made available for Chrissie with, for example, her GP, as it will take longer for her to express her needs.

- Advise Chrissie on actions that can be taken if she experiences any discrimination, and make complaints with her or on her behalf.

(d) Example content may include:

Emma's employer has a responsibility to ensure she:
- understands how to implement their codes of practice
- has a line manager (a social worker) who has responsibility for her, who Emma can turn to for advice and support
- meets National Occupational Standards (NOS)
- undertakes continuing professional development (CPD)
- is safeguarded through being able to have internal/external complaints dealt with properly
- is safeguarded by being able to take part in whistleblowing
- is safeguarded by having membership of a trade union and/or professional association (HCPC)
- is safeguarded by following the protocols of regulatory bodies
- is protected by having policies and procedures in place, so Emma implements best practice to meet needs while working within the law
- is protected by having guidelines in place designed to keep her safe at work.

**3** (a) Example content may include:

The Disclosure and Barring Service (DBS) carries out checks on whether a person:
- has a criminal record
- has anything in their past/background that suggests they are a possible risk to others
- is on a list of people barred from doing the role.

(b) Example content may include:
- Make sure everyone understands how important it is to keep children safe.
- Make sure all the agencies/service providers that are part of the LSCB are doing the best job.
- Develop policies and procedures for safeguarding and promoting the welfare of children.
- Identify the action to be taken where there are concerns about a child's safety or welfare.
- Develop guidelines on the training of people who work with people, or in services, where the safety and welfare of children must be taken into account.
- Develop guidelines on the recruitment and supervision of people who work with children.
- Report to the Department of Health.
- Look into cases where children are badly hurt or have died, and report on lessons learned.
- Give advice to all service providers to help them work in partnership to protect children.
- Listen to children's ideas and views.
- Participate in the planning of services for children in the area.

(c) Example content may include:
- Ensure the visiting area is safe, for example, that it is neat and tidy with no trip or slip hazards.
- Talk to the visitor to find out who they are visiting, so they can be directed to the right place rather than wandering round disturbing other patients and visitors.
- Provide support to the visitor according to their needs, for example, if they are worried or distressed offer words of reassurance or comfort.
- Ensure that any information given to the visitor is accurate, so mistakes aren't made, such as directing the visitor to the wrong ward which would waste the visitor's time.
- Maintain confidentiality by making sure that their conversation with the visitor cannot be overheard by others.
- Seek help if unable to deal with the visitor, for example, if they cannot provide the information that is needed.
- Listen carefully to, and communicate well with, the visitor, so there can be no misunderstanding or mistakes.

(d) Example content may include:
- Prepare care plans that are appropriate for Jasmine's needs, with support identified and provided so that the plans can be carried out.
- Ensure Jasmine's care meets her physical needs, so ensuring access to the medication and procedures she needs.
- Ensure Jasmine's care reflects hers and her family's preferences, so they all feel involved and valued.
- Enable Jasmine to access all the services she needs, working in partnership and adopting a holistic approach, so as many of her needs as possible are met.
- Help Jasmine's parents obtain suitable equipment for Jasmine, such as a motorised wheelchair, to help Jasmine be more independent.
- Arrange for necessary adaptations to Jasmine's home, such as a bathroom that accommodates her wheelchair, so her parents can help her with day-to-day tasks such as washing.
- Help her parents access benefits so one or both of them doesn't/don't need to work and can look after her.
- Ensure that respite care is available when her parents need a rest.
- Help the family cope with adjustments to normal living.
- Make sure Jasmine is kept safe, whether it be at home, at the hospital or at school.
- Ensure a healthy environment, so Jasmine does not catch any infections.
- Encourage her learning and development, including play, making sure Jasmine does not fall too far behind her peers.
- Ensure her welfare is paramount, so comfort and reassure her when she is upset or feeling ill.
- Ensure that information about Jasmine remains confidential.
- Provide information to keep Jasmine's family fully informed about her care and involved in any decisions about her care.

4   (a) Example content may include:
- To have fair and equal treatment from all the staff.
- To be consulted about his care.
- To be consulted about his preferences, such as going out on the trips on offer.
- To be protected from harm and risk.
- To have his personal data kept safe and secure.

(b) Example content may include:

> A care home manager does not need to register with the HCPC unless they are a social worker. Most care home managers are not social workers. They must be registered as the manager with the CQC.

- The Care Quality Commission (CQC) if in England/The Care and Social Services Inspectorate Wales (CSSIW)/The Regulation and Quality Improvement Authority (RQIA) in Northern Ireland regulates my work.
- I have to follow the regulations and codes of professional conduct set out by professional bodies.
- I have to be familiar with, and be able to apply, current codes of practice.
- I have to be registered with a professional body.
- My work and that of my staff will be inspected as part of external inspections by professional bodies such as The Care Quality Commission (CQC) in England/The Care and Social Services Inspectorate Wales (CSSIW)/The Regulation and Quality Improvement Authority (RQIA) in Northern Ireland.
- As part of the inspection process my work will be observed and service users will be asked their opinion.
- I have to make sure my staff are properly trained and can also follow regulations, codes of practice, codes of professional conduct and are registered by a professional body.

(c) Example content may include:
The local authority will have considered whether Bill's needs:
- arose from, or were related to, a physical or mental impairment or illness
- made him unable to achieve two or more of the specified outcomes which are:
  o maintain personal and home hygiene
  o go to the toilet appropriately
  o get dressed/dress appropriately
  o move around inside and outside safely
  o access personal relationships to avoid loneliness
  o access occupations such as work, training or volunteering
  o use local facilities and transport
  o prepare and eat food and drink
  o care for others
- impacted significantly on his wellbeing as a result of being unable to meet these outcomes.
Bill was eligible for personal care because he met all three criteria due to his lack of mobility.

(d) Example content may include:
I would:
- make sure there are enough appropriately trained care assistants on duty at all times to keep residents such as Bill safe from falling when he needs, for example, to go to the toilet, as he may be tempted to go on his own if there are no staff available, so increasing his risk of falls
- use risk assessments to identify possible sources of harm to Bill, and assess the likelihood of them causing harm, to minimise the risks of him sustaining an injury
- support Bill to manage risks, for example, ask care assistants to train him how to get up from his chair while he holds onto his walker firmly and securely with the brakes on, to reduce the risk of falls
- provide equipment so that care assistants can move Bill safely, for example, provide hoists to lift him in and out of the bath
- encourage Bill to keep joining in with activities, such as trips out in the minibus, and to walk with his walker rather than resort to using a wheelchair to get around the home, so he maintains his mobility as long as possible
- provide medications where necessary to keep Bill free from joint pain and so enable him to be active and mobile
- arrange access to other services, such as physiotherapy, to keep Bill as mobile as possible
- expect the care assistants to encourage Bill to join in exercise programmes, even if it is armchair exercises, to help keep his joints mobile
- provide a healthy diet and expect care assistants to make sure Bill eats his meals, so he does not become obese and lose more mobility
- provide maintained first aid facilities so that if Bill does have a fall he can be treated as quickly as possible, so reducing the risk of any permanent damage
- provide a rigorous reports and complaints procedure, so all incidents are reported and investigated straight away and potential sources of risk removed before residents such as Bill have an accident which leads to reduced mobility and activity
- make sure there are appropriate policies and procedures, including whistleblowing, in place to keep Bill safe and as active and mobile as possible
- provide induction and CPD to make sure all care assistants are up to date with all regulations, policies and procedures.

# Notes

# Notes

# Notes

# Notes